STRENGTH TRAINING
for Performance Driving

Mark Martin, NASCAR Driver

John S. Comereski, M.A.T., Trainer/Exercise Physiologist

Motorbooks International
Publishers & Wholesalers ®

To the two most influential people in my life—
my mother, Josephine,
and my father, Lawrence (deceased).
—John S. Comereski

First published in 1994 by Motorbooks International Publishers & Wholesalers, PO Box 2, 729 Prospect Avenue, Osceola, WI 54020 USA

Library of Congress Cataloging-in-Publication Data

Martin, Mark.
    Strength training for performance driving / Mark Martin, John S. Comereski.
       p. cm.
    Includes index.
    ISBN 0-87938-843-9
      1. Automobile racing—Training. 2. Weight lifting. 3. Physical fitness. I. Comereski, John S. II. Title.
GV1029.M26   1994
796.7'2—dc20   93-21106

On the front cover:
Main photo: Co-author and NASCAR driver Mark Martin poses with his Roush Racing Valvoline Thunderbird. *Dan R. Boyd*
Insets: Co-authors Mark Martin and John S. Comereski work out. *Jeff Terpack*

On the back cover: The co-authors in the weight room, and Mark Martin performing a curl. *Jeff Terpack*

Printed and bound in the United States of America

Contents

Acknowledgments

The authors sincerely wish to thank all of those who provided significant contributions in the preparation of this book. We are indebted to many fine individuals. They include Josephine Comereski, who spent hours upon hours on this project, as well as Joseph McGrane and Pamela Shuart for their patience in editing the manuscript. Thanks also to Jay Wilcox, Frank Morich, Ken Bates, and Smith Paulison for offering their expertise in racing. To Joe Weider, Weider Health & Fitness, and Fred Hatfield, Ph. D., director of the International Sports Sciences Association, for his sound advice on exercise and nutrition.

For their input on professional racing, we offer our sincere gratitude to Steve Kinser, thirteen-time World of Outlaws Champion, known as the "King of the Outlaws" and current driver of the #11 Valvoline sprint car; Chip Hanauer, seven-time Unlimited Hydroplane National Champion and current driver of the Ms. Budweiser Hydroplane; Ron Magruder, sponsorship coordinator and originator of the "Big Foot" Monster Truck; Steve Hmiel, crew chief of the #6 Valvoline Ford Thunderbird NASCAR Winston Cup car; and Joe Amato, 1992 NHRA Winston Top Fuel Dragster World Champion. We wish continued success to these fine athletes.

We'd like to offer a special thanks to Lindel Estes, the president of the Mark Martin Fan Club; Jay Frye, sports marketing coordinator for Valvoline Inc.; Diane Hollingsworth of Roush Racing; and Connie Antilley, public relations for NASCAR. They each helped to provide valuable information toward the writing of this book.

Our thanks also go out to ASICS TIGER Corporation for providing us with our fine athletic apparel, and Salvatore Princiotto and Howard Johnson Motor Lodge, Horseheads, New York, for allowing us to use a hotel room for our "On the Road" exercise recommendations.

In addition, we thank photographer Bryan Hallman for the action-packed photographs of the #6 Folgers Ford Thunderbird accident that occurred at Talladega in 1991. And a big thanks to Jeff Terpack, whose patience was far beyond ours in photographing and preparing all the exercise and stretching photos. His endless hours of work on this project are well appreciated and acknowledged.

Last but not least, we would like to extend our appreciation to Marc Rubin Associates for their time and efforts spent in designing our book cover.

Without the help of these wonderful people, *Strength Training for Performance Driving* would not be the quality book it is today.

—*Mark Martin*
—*John S. Comereski*

Preface

At no time in the history of man have exercise and nutrition had such prominence as they have today. Not only are they essential for healthy living, but they are also necessary in the successful pursuit of improved physical performance on the job, at home, and on the racetrack.

Today all racing teams—whether automobile, boat, motorcycle, or all-terrain vehicle racing—are seeking ways to improve performance both by increasing vehicle speed and by improving the drivers' racing ability. More and more attention is being focused on the latter, and thus to the physical conditioning of drivers and pit crew members. To have a well-conditioned team means improving overall race performance on the track and in the pits, along with keeping the entire team healthy throughout the race season.

You do not have to be an avid racer to benefit from this book. Whether you are interested in improving your ability to drive your own car, protect against injury while working on your car, or even if you just want to know how to exercise correctly, you will find it informative. Whatever your interest, *Strength Training for Performance Driving* can help in your quest for physical greatness.

Everyone who partakes in the game of iron wants to get the most out of what he or she is doing. For a racing enthusiast who doesn't want to "waste time" exercising, scientifically sound techniques are constantly being sought. It's not necessarily true that those educated in the physiological sciences know the *practical aspects* of physical training, yet combining their theories with a sound hands-on approach allows one to achieve the best outcomes.

Several options are available for those seeking exercise information: spend lots of time reading a slew of controversial materials; waste more time learning through trial and error; take advice from some musclehead whose achievements might be evident despite unproductive practices; or learn from those who have both the knowledge and the experience. This book combines both knowledge and experience to help readers learn the proper ways to be the best they can be.

The future of motorsports depends on improvements in technology along with improvements in human performance. Improved performance can be attributed to strength training, proper dietary habits, stress control, and adequate rest.

Simply put, to be your best, you need the best information, and you'll get the best information here.

Chapter 1

The Connection

With good physical fitness, the body becomes less likely to become fatigued and subsequently less likely to commit errors. Errors that can cost you a race, injury, or even your life.

With good physical fitness, the body becomes less likely to become fatigued and subsequently less likely to commit errors—errors that can cost you a race, an injury, or even your life.

In the world of motorsports, speed is always the major concern. Seldom is adequate emphasis given to the driver or pit crew, who make that speed happen. As in any other physically and mentally draining activity, racing demands physical conditioning efforts from its participants. To maintain a high intensity of driving ability and to make positive split-second decisions, a healthy, strong body is required.

The conditioning information in this book focuses on, but is not restricted to, physical demands placed on motorsports enthusiasts who participate in events such as these:
• Car racing (including stock cars, drag racers, Indy cars, road rallying, and karts)
• Truck racing (including drag racing and off-road events)
• Speedboat racing (including hydroplanes)
• Motorcycle racing (including motocross, drags, and road racing events)
• ATV (all-terrain vehicle) racing (including three- and four- wheelers, snowmobiles, and personal watercraft)

You can train your body to do almost anything. Your body reacts to stimulus by finding ways to adapt to it. So goes it for strength training. Your body adapts to the physical demands your conditioning places on it by becoming stronger. But this does not reflect muscle strength only; it includes a host of other additional benefits.

Among the goals of this book are to direct you to greater strength and make you less prone to fatigue and its resulting errors. Yet the benefits of strength training reach much further than that, possibly further than you might have ever imagined. By following a strength training program you can not only increase your strength but also:
• nurture proper joint alignment
• strengthen your bones
• improve your blood flow and reduce blood pressure
• increase flexibility
• enhance coordination and speed reaction time
• let you sleep better and
• reduce the stress load in your life

Sound miraculous? Perhaps, yet it's all possible through a commitment to a practical strength training program. In this chapter, we'll focus on the physical changes and benefits strength training can produce, while in chapter 2 we'll look at performance benefits that are possible.

What follows are some of the most pronounced physical improvements that you as a racer can achieve through a properly designed and implemented strength training program.

1.1 Muscular Benefits

You should have no doubts that strength training makes your skeletal muscles stronger and improves muscular endurance. But what you may not realize is that muscle tone achieved through proper strength training better also prepares your muscles for quick action. To a strong driver faced with split-second decision making, this means faster reaction time.

Here's what it looks like to travel 160mph, as author Mark Martin did when he won the 1992 Mello Yello 500 at Charlotte Motor Speedway. That blur just to the left of *the start-finish line is Mark's No. 6 Valvoline Thunderbird.*

Whether you hold onto a steering wheel for hours at a time or simply grasp handlebars for a 5- to 10-minute moto, shoulders and arms that are weak will fatigue early, making racing a more strenuous event than it needs to be. Just imagine how much work is involved in steering a hydroplane that is propelled by 3700hp engines, weighs in at roughly 6,000 pounds (lb), and travels upward of 200mph. Not an easy task.

Keep in mind that strength training not only strengthens your muscles, but it also makes for stronger tendons. Tendons are the structures that connect muscles to bone. And when muscles contract with great force, much of the force is passed along to the connecting tendons. For the racer who has well-conditioned muscles and tendons, the risk of tendinitis is greatly reduced. This is especially true for the driver who grips his or her steering wheel or handlebars with clenched hands. Even with a relaxed grip, the repetitive movement of steering a vehicle can lead to irritated and inflamed tendons. "Tennis elbow" is a common affliction experienced in such events, even in the absence of playing tennis.

When a motocross racer rounds a corner during a race, the muscles of the legs help support the racer's body weight along with partial weight of the motorcycle coupled together with centrifugal force (force that tends to impel the cycle outward throughout the cornering). And although it is apparent the leg muscles are working hard, it is less evident, but nevertheless important, that the muscles of the midsection and upper body are also providing stability through the turn.

Every movement that you perform during and in preparation for racing is a distinct product of muscle contraction. Even though an action may not require maximal forces, strength training allows you to perform submaximal strength movements with increasing ease and speed.

1.2 Types of Muscles

Your body consists of three types of muscles: involuntary (smooth) muscles which act by themselves; voluntary (skeletal) muscles which respond at your will; and the cardiac muscle, which is your heart.

As you participate in certain regimens of strength training (such as circuit training), the involuntary muscles become conditioned. These are the muscles lining your blood vessels and your digestive tract. Such exercise stimulates these mus-

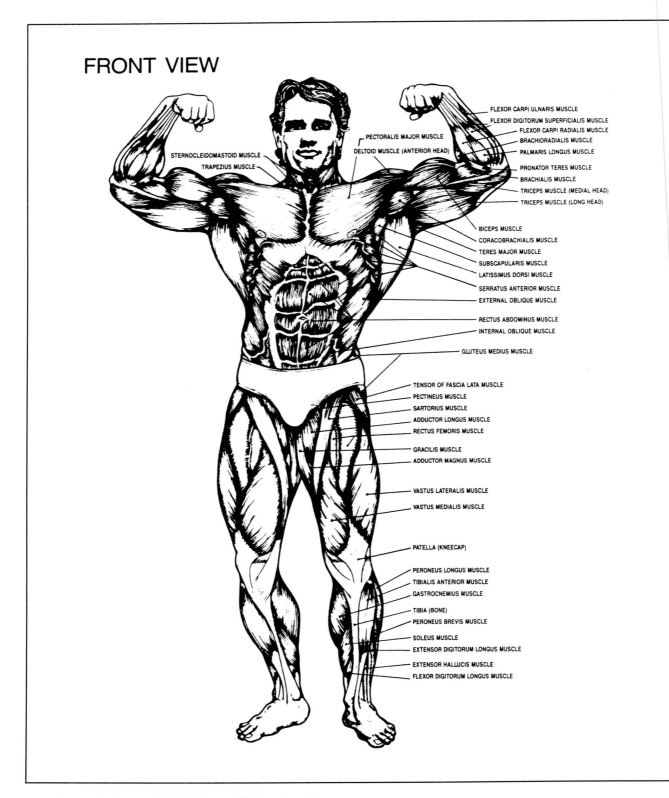

FRONT VIEW

STERNOCLEIDOMASTOID MUSCLE
TRAPEZIUS MUSCLE

PECTORALIS MAJOR MUSCLE
DELTOID MUSCLE (ANTERIOR HEAD)

FLEXOR CARPI ULNARIS MUSCLE
FLEXOR DIGITORUM SUPERFICIALIS MUSCLE
FLEXOR CARPI RADIALIS MUSCLE
BRACHIORADIALIS MUSCLE
PALMARIS LONGUS MUSCLE
PRONATOR TERES MUSCLE
BRACHIALIS MUSCLE
TRICEPS MUSCLE (MEDIAL HEAD)
TRICEPS MUSCLE (LONG HEAD)

BICEPS MUSCLE
CORACOBRACHIALIS MUSCLE
TERES MAJOR MUSCLE
SUBSCAPULARIS MUSCLE
LATISSIMUS DORSI MUSCLE
SERRATUS ANTERIOR MUSCLE
EXTERNAL OBLIQUE MUSCLE

RECTUS ABDOMINUS MUSCLE
INTERNAL OBLIQUE MUSCLE

GLUTEUS MEDIUS MUSCLE

TENSOR OF FASCIA LATA MUSCLE
PECTINEUS MUSCLE
SARTORIUS MUSCLE
ADDUCTOR LONGUS MUSCLE
RECTUS FEMORIS MUSCLE

GRACILIS MUSCLE
ADDUCTOR MAGNUS MUSCLE

VASTUS LATERALIS MUSCLE

VASTUS MEDIALIS MUSCLE

PATELLA (KNEECAP)

PERONEUS LONGUS MUSCLE
TIBIALIS ANTERIOR MUSCLE
GASTROCNEMIUS MUSCLE

TIBIA (BONE)
PERONEUS BREVIS MUSCLE

SOLEUS MUSCLE
EXTENSOR DIGITORUM LONGUS MUSCLE

EXTENSOR HALLUCIS MUSCLE
FLEXOR DIGITORUM LONGUS MUSCLE

Muscles in the human body. These will be referred to throughout the text, in both their medical and common terms, so use these charts to locate muscles and muscle groups being described in discussions of stretches, exercises, and workouts.

BACK VIEW

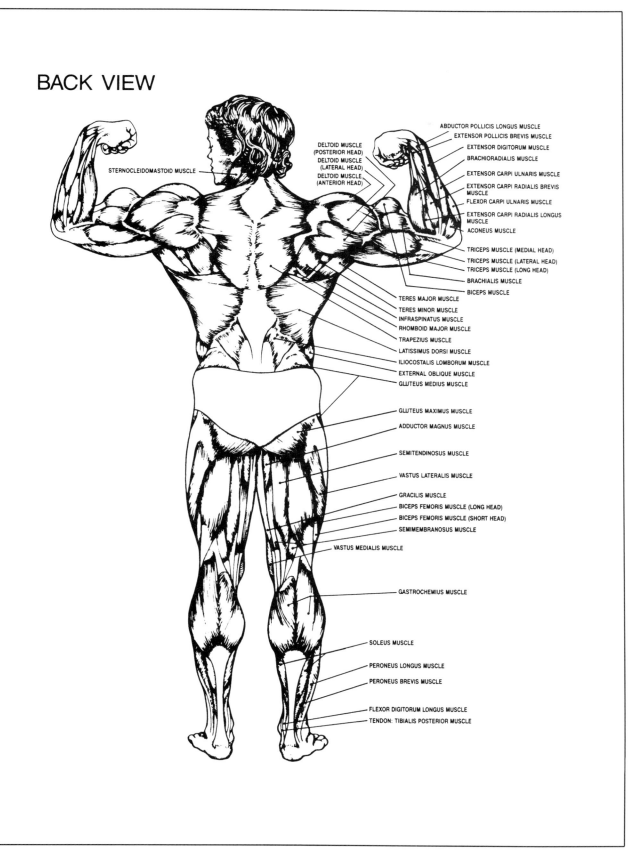

STERNOCLEIDOMASTOID MUSCLE

DELTOID MUSCLE
(POSTERIOR HEAD)
DELTOID MUSCLE
(LATERAL HEAD)
DELTOID MUSCLE
(ANTERIOR HEAD)

ABDUCTOR POLLICIS LONGUS MUSCLE
EXTENSOR POLLICIS BREVIS MUSCLE
EXTENSOR DIGITORUM MUSCLE
BRACHIORADIALIS MUSCLE
EXTENSOR CARPI ULNARIS MUSCLE
EXTENSOR CARPI RADIALIS BREVIS
MUSCLE
FLEXOR CARPI ULNARIS MUSCLE
EXTENSOR CARPI RADIALIS LONGUS
MUSCLE
ACONEUS MUSCLE

TRICEPS MUSCLE (MEDIAL HEAD)
TRICEPS MUSCLE (LATERAL HEAD)
TRICEPS MUSCLE (LONG HEAD)
BRACHIALIS MUSCLE
BICEPS MUSCLE

TERES MAJOR MUSCLE
TERES MINOR MUSCLE
INFRASPINATUS MUSCLE
RHOMBOID MAJOR MUSCLE
TRAPEZIUS MUSCLE
LATISSIMUS DORSI MUSCLE
ILIOCOSTALIS LOMBORUM MUSCLE
EXTERNAL OBLIQUE MUSCLE
GLUTEUS MEDIUS MUSCLE

GLUTEUS MAXIMUS MUSCLE
ADDUCTOR MAGNUS MUSCLE
SEMITENDINOSUS MUSCLE
VASTUS LATERALIS MUSCLE
GRACILIS MUSCLE
BICEPS FEMORIS MUSCLE (LONG HEAD)
BICEPS FEMORIS MUSCLE (SHORT HEAD)
SEMIMEMBRANOSUS MUSCLE

VASTUS MEDIALIS MUSCLE

GASTROCHEMIUS MUSCLE

SOLEUS MUSCLE

PERONEUS LONGUS MUSCLE

PERONEUS BREVIS MUSCLE

FLEXOR DIGITORUM LONGUS MUSCLE
TENDON: TIBIALIS POSTERIOR MUSCLE

cles to contract with greater force. This allows, among other things, greater blood flow to various tissues (muscles, organs, and so on) and improved digestion of food. These muscles also become more capable of relaxing. This is so indicated in the blood vessels with conditions like hypertension (high blood pressure). Through such a training effect, high levels of pressure within your arteries decline. To some individuals, this can mean a reduction or cessation in blood pressure medication.

In addition, the cardiac muscle strengthens and becomes more efficient with both increased stroke volume (amount of blood pumped with each heart contraction or beat) and reduced resting heart rate. This subsequently places less of a demand on your heart during rest and vigorous activity.

For you the racer, involuntary muscle conditioning is important because it allows you to perform for longer periods before feeling fatigued. That is why well-trained athletes fatigue less easily.

To understand the importance of voluntary muscle conditioning, you must first realize how your muscles become stronger. Muscles contract because of the action of the contractile proteins within your muscle cells. When the concentration of these proteins rises, your muscles get stronger. Through progressive resistance training (also known as strength training), the overload, which submits your muscles to increasingly greater workloads, creates a need for contractile proteins to be manufactured. As this need is tended to by your muscles, each protein filament becomes thicker while additional protein filaments are added. Although other microscopic changes occur during such exercise, these are the major adjustments made to allow for greater strength.

Strengthening your skeletal muscles should be a major concern of anyone having anything to do with racing and performance driving. We cannot emphasize this enough! The stronger the muscle tissue, the greater the outside forces required for it to become injured. And basically, stronger muscles resist some outside forces that would otherwise cause them to strain or tear.

Weak neck muscles lead to a weak cervical spine, while weak lower back muscles can lead to all-too-common back pain. Just imagine, if you will, what it's like to drive a race car on an oval track for hours on end while supporting your 15lb head with your neck muscles. Strap on a full-face helmet and the neck's burden increases. Even though you have a headrest helping you, what's to lower your risk of whiplash when getting hit broadside? Strong neck muscles—that's what!

To be muscularly fit is to have substantial lean muscle mass, muscular strength and endurance, and quick reaction time. This is the foundation on which strength training for performance driving is based. Increased strength and muscle tone better prepare you to handle stresses placed on your muscles, whether they be from the weights or from the vehicle you're driving.

In addition, a balance of muscle strength in your body is required for maintaining proper bone alignment and guarding against joint injury. It is often the case that those who display poor posture are at high risk for injury. Such an imbalance of muscular strength (and, most likely, flexibility) can be the direct or indirect cause of injury. And it's more common than you may think.

Most of us have at one time or another experienced misalignment of the vertebrae. Oftentimes, a trip to the chiropractor is a source of relief through the manipulation of bones into their proper alignment.

When such an imbalance of muscle strength is present, or when muscles lack elasticity (flexibility), outside forces to a joint are often absorbed by the body's structure or to the weaker muscles. This can result in injury to the muscles, tendons, ligaments, bones, or cartilage present in the joints. It's like a monster truck hitting the ground after being airborne. If it lands on all four wheels, it's less likely to become damaged, but if the weight of the truck lands on one wheel, damage to the truck's suspension is highly probable.

For the human body, similar but smaller stresses can result in either a more even distribution of forces within the joints (proper alignment) or excessive segmental forces (improper alignment). The latter is an injury waiting to happen.

Perhaps you are in agreement with several of the uninformed sources that swimming is the best form of exercise because it involves the body's major muscle groups. While swimming has its place in competition and leisure time activity, it can lead to muscle imbalance. For example, the chest and back muscles pulling the arms downward during a stroke work much harder than the shoulder muscles moving the arms forward through the air. The strength of the chest and back muscles can overpower the shoulder muscles, and an imbalance of shoulder strength then arises. This can result in damage to the deep shoulder muscles collectively called the rotator cuff.

The protection that strength training offers is evident in the accident experienced by racer Mark Martin at Talladega in 1991. If an imbalance of muscle strength was present in Mark's back or neck, spinal injury likely would have occurred.

1.3 Increasing Muscular Strength and Endurance

Your muscular endurance increases when you become stronger. This allows your performance to be less physically demanding. Yet when racing situations become intense, you are prepared to handle them. This is a bit more complex, however, than you may think.

Increases in strength, local muscle endurance, and strength endurance are well established by-products of properly performed strength training. Providing your strength training is done correctly, your ability to perform less-than-maximal muscular contractions over a prolonged period (local muscle endurance) improves, along with your ability to display maximal muscular contractions time after time (strength endurance).

Muscular endurance allows you to reproduce good performance without late-race fatigue. Simply stated, you maintain your strength levels throughout an entire lengthy race.

And for those involved in the likes of sprint car, speedboat, and drag racing, this muscular endurance is needed throughout race day as several heats of racing may be required.

1.4 Tendons and Ligaments

At each end of every muscle is a tendon connected to bones. Tendons are made of thick, white tissue and possess little elasticity. Any bodily movement, whether turning a vehicle, putting on a tire, or simply lifting a weight, is begun with a muscle contraction that pulls on the tendons, which in turn pull on the bones, and thus moves the skeletal system.

Ligaments, on the other hand, attach bone to bone, holding joints together. These are thinner and less elastic than tendons, and are white. The white color of tendons and ligaments reflects the low blood supply they receive. If you look at a muscle chart that's illustrated in color, you'll notice the tendons (and ligaments, if so illustrated) as white tissues. By comparison, muscle tissue is red (in color) due to a higher blood supply. Surprising to some, even bones have a greater blood supply serving them than do tendons or ligaments. Generally speaking, the higher the blood supply, the more elasticity present in the tendons and ligaments. Inactivity leads to a loss of tissue elasticity just as the aging process does, due in part, to a lack of a blood supply. This helps explain, then, why injured tendons and ligaments take so long to recover from injury.

Since force is placed on the tendons during any movement or muscle contraction, weak tendons can become strained, torn, inflamed (tendinitis), or even separated from the attached bone or muscle. And if outside forces compel a joint to move beyond its normal range of motion, injury in the form of a sprain occurs. Fortunately, tendons and ligaments also adapt to strength training by becoming stronger and developing an increased blood supply.

1.5 Blood Flow

By now, it should be obvious that strength training has a dramatic effect on blood flow to and from your tissues. This benefit is apparent not only during exercise, but also while at rest. Because improved blood flow increases the availability of nutrient-rich blood reaching damaged tissues, this is an important matter during recovery from exercise and injury. And when waste products accumulate soon after exercise (such as carbon dioxide, for example) or injury (dead blood cells), increased blood flow speeds up the necessary removal of these substances.

1.6 Nerve-Muscle Interaction

Nerves connect to your muscles and carry electrical impulses to the muscles, causing them to contract. Although more complex, your nerves resemble the electrical wires of your car that carry electrical messages to the spark plugs (the muscles) from the distributor (the brain).

To move a body part, your brain sends an electrical signal via your central nervous system (your spinal cord) to the nerves connecting various muscles. This, in turn, stimulates your muscles to contract.

The effectiveness of this nerve-muscle (neuromuscular) function improves through regular strength training. As a result, your muscles respond faster and with greater force. Here's the physiology behind it all: As you become stronger, your nerves become more easily excitable or stimulated to send messages to the muscles to contract. This leads to a greater degree of nerve stimulation and therefore increased force output (strength). However, your body has defense mechanisms protecting your muscles from tearing themselves apart.

Sensory receptors (also called proprioceptors), which are sensitive to stretch, tension, or pain, send a message to your nervous system when a muscle is under too much tension (golgi tendon organs) or stretched too far (muscle spindles). Intense strength training readjusts the thresholds at which these mechanisms signal your brain to "shut down" muscular work due to excessive tension or stretch. The result is greater strength and flexibility.

If you are racing at 100-plus mph your reactions to situations must be quick—instinctively quick, in fact. By training your muscles to produce force at a fast rate, you improve your reaction time. This element of performance will then depend upon your decision making.

As with any muscle movement, improved reaction time is a learned trait. You learn to walk by attempting it time and time again until your coordination allows you to do so. And whatever your physical endeavor, it all takes coordination. To get a better understanding of this, place yourself in this scenario: In a race car you are required to shift gears with your right hand. Have you ever tried shifting gears with your left hand? (If you try this, make sure you're sitting where a passenger would be.) We're sure you cannot be as deliberate nor as fast in doing so. This, performance driving friends, requires coordination, and hopefully you have learned it well. (You'll find further discussion of coordination in Chapter 2 as well.)

Contrary to a once popular myth that you either have coordination or you don't, it has been proven that you *can* improve your coordination. Body movements are simply the function of your nerves and muscles, and your control over them can be improved upon. Skills training (fine motor skills) for performance driving can be enhanced through strength training by teaching your body to quickly "turn on" certain muscles and shut off others, all with precise timing. In any type of racing, literally dozens of stimulated muscle contractions are involved in a unique series of movements (coordination) like turning a wheel or handlebars, stepping on the brake or accelerator, mounting a tire, or bending sheet metal.

There's an old saying: Practice makes perfect. But this is true only if the practice is done perfectly. In fact, it is far more appropriate to say: Practice makes habit. If your skills training in and on your race or high-performance vehicle is complemented by properly performed strength training, your ability to race or drive well improves. On the other hand, incorrect practices in either driving or strength training can result in injury.

Performance benefits of strength training in racing can be thought of like this: You can be skillful at racing, but if you don't have the strength to effectively repeat these skills throughout a race, you are likely to finish in poor position with an increased chance of injury from crashing. Posting a pole-winning one-lap time is one thing, but driving hard for 500 laps is another thing all together.

1.7 Maintaining Proper Joint Status

When bones become misaligned, pain often results. Weak and inflexible muscles are frequently the culprits. The race driver with misaligned vertebrae of the lower back finds himself with great discomfort and consequently less than optimal performance.

By strengthening the muscles surrounding the joints, you lower the chances of misalignment occurring. The muscles include not only those directly supporting the structure, but also those assisting in the support. For example, you need to condition the small muscles connecting the vertebrae; however, your large back muscles along with the abdominals must also be strong. This combination of strong muscle groups helps maintain proper

alignment of the lumbar or lower spine, which is then capable of withstanding greater stresses generated to these small joints before injury occurs.

Imagine the discomfort felt by a NASCAR (National Association for Stock Car Automobile Racing) driver suffering from back pain resulting from misaligned vertebrae. Keep in mind that this driver spends hours of intense concentration and split-second decision making, often at speeds in excess of 150mph, all while sitting—securely harnessed—in a single position. It's easy to see why such a driver with misaligned vertebrae would be far less than prepared for all-out racing.

1.8 Improving Body Composition

Do you realize how much time and effort go into reducing the weight of a racing vehicle by even 10lb? Sure, there are minimum weight limits in some forms of racing, but mechanics and crews prefer to distribute the weight where it is most beneficial rather than where it has to be.

If you think about it, what if you were able to reduce the combined weight of the car and driver by 10lb? Doesn't it make sense that the vehicle would run faster? Of course it does. Only a fool would deny this.

Then why not reduce the weight that the vehicle must carry during a race? It's a good idea, but this matter presents itself as a double-bladed sword. If the driver's body weight is too light, he or she will not likely be strong and will thus carry a higher risk of injury. The major concern here is the driver's strength-to-weight ratio. Usually, the stronger the body, the bigger it is and the less likely it is to become injured. The key is to have a lean body (low body fat) that is strong. With this in mind, you can see how body composition plays an important role in the total racing picture.

Strength training is the best means of improving body composition—period. This encompasses the increase in lean body mass with a concomitant decrease in body fat. Everyone knows that strength training increases the strength and weight of your bones and muscles. But unbeknown to several of our exercise gurus, strength training helps reduce unwanted body fat in two major ways.

First, it burns calories while you are training (acute effect). Recent research shows that although your metabolism remains elevated to a higher degree (and thus burns more calories) during aerobic exercise as compared to strength training, it returns to resting levels soon afterward. A metabolism that is elevated during strength training remains elevated for roughly thirty minutes afterward. Total caloric expenditure, including recovery periods, is therefore similar for both types of exercise.

Second, as you increase lean body mass through strength training, your metabolism remains elevated even at rest (chronic effect), although not to the same level as during exercise. You therefore burn more calories at whatever you do.

1.9 Bone Strengthening

If you drive or watch speedboat racers bounce around atop the water, you can see the repetitive forces that are generated to the body. Some forces are minor, while some are intense. Regardless of the severity, this jarring can easily produce stress fractures or even complete fractures of weak bones.

A multitude of research studies show that strength training increases the strength of your bones to a much greater degree than any other activity. In fact, when the bone density of various athletes is compared, it is the weight lifters who have the strongest bones.

With this in mind, you can see the built-in safety benefits of strength training for participants in the motorsports game. Obviously, strength training and the resulting bone strengthening reduce the chances of fractures resulting from accidents. Another benefit is the reduced risk of stress fractures that can result from overuse, as in the case of series racing every weekend for several consecutive weeks. And for those susceptible to osteoporosis (guys, this isn't a disease that affects women only), strength training significantly reduces this risk.

Bone is not an unchanging structure. Surprised? You shouldn't be. Bone is a living tissue of the body that throughout life is constantly being broken down and rebuilt on a microscopic level.

Here's how it works: Bone has a life cycle of about four months. This means that all bone is broken down and rebuilt within this period. Initiating this cycle are the demolition cells referred to as osteoclasts, which virtually demineralize bone. When the function of the osteoclasts is completed,

osteoblasts (bone-producing cells) move in and lay down protein-building materials (osteoproteins) in the sites where demineralization has occurred. The osteoproteins combine with calcium to eventually harden and become new bone. This process is known as calcification.

As will be stated time and time again, strength training is the very best means of strengthening your bones. When a muscle is under stress, it in turn places tension on the attached bones. This tension creates an electrical force inside the bones, causing a stimulation of osteoblast activity. Together with increased blood supply, the osteoblast activity forces you to become stronger. But keep in mind: If strength training ceases, your bones will gradually return to a weaker state.

Although some forms of aerobic training like cycling and running have elicited increased bone density, these changes occur only in the bones connected to the working muscles. And since strength training allows you to select the body parts to be strengthened, no other form of exercise can compare to its specific benefits for racers and other performance drivers. You can pick and choose which bones you wish to strengthen. Perhaps we should concern ourselves with those bones which are most commonly fractured during racing mishaps. For Indy circuit racers, this could mean a heavy concentration on lower leg strengthening, since there is a high incidence of lower leg fractures among these drivers.

It is obvious that stronger bones handle greater forces before they break. With this in mind, you may ask yourself the same question we have been asking ourselves for years: Since nearly every racer has had at least one broken bone, then why doesn't everyone in racing participate in strength training? Well, fellow race fans, it's usually a case of laziness and/or lack of information. Hopefully, this book will stimulate the couch potatoes of racing to get up and get into the gym.

Chapter 2

Strength Training: A Necessity, Not a Hobby

In racing, where the focus has long been on drawing peak performance from a machine, drivers and their crews have a growing concern for peak physical and mental performances. Their interest and efforts toward this end will make racing a safer and more successful endeavor.

In racing—where drivers, mechanics, and pit crews strive to achieve peak performance from their machines—there's a growing concern for peak physical and mental performances from each individual involved. This interest in improving bodily capabilities will contribute to making racing and performance driving safer and more successful.

High-performance setups in all racing cars, trucks, boats, motorcycles, and all-terrain vehicles are crucial to success in racing. Until now, however, seldom has much, if any, consideration been given to the "high performance abilities" of the racer. You can have the fastest car on the NASCAR or Indy circuit, but if you are not capable of driving it intensely, without becoming unduly fatigued, you might as well stay home.

Strength and fitness advocates have long been puzzled about why the two worlds of fitness and racing did not come together sooner. It only makes sense—a driver who is more fit gets the most out of his or her vehicle. And since the most important *serious* consideration in any sporting activity, especially racing, is the prevention of injury, action should be taken to reduce the risks.

As noted earlier, the human body adapts in numerous ways to strength training. We have chosen to discuss those adaptations that have the greatest effect upon racing and high-performance driving skills. We'll focus on those effects that are most pronounced and most beneficial.

Obviously, stronger tissues are more resistant to outside forces that might injure them. Thus, injury prevention is a benefit. But not so obvious is the fact that the benefits of strength training are not limited to creating stronger muscles. What follows are some of the major benefits derived from a strength training program.

2.1 Increase in Flexibility

The true consideration of flexibility not only concerns the range of motion of a joint, but also strength in the extreme ranges of motion. This is what actually protects your joints from becoming injured. And this can only be accomplished through proper strength training.

When an accident takes place, injury most often occurs to the body that is restricted and, in a sense, "tight." Take an intoxicated driver, for instance. When a person in such a state is involved in an auto accident, he or she seldom gets injured, because he or she is "loose" and gives with the movement of the vehicle. Similarly, a fit racer who "gives" with the movement when involved in an accident has a reduced chance of being injured. Perhaps this is the time a driver must rely on safety mechanisms of the vehicle (such as a roll bar). However, a stronger body can absorb more shocking forces without "breaking" or becoming injured.

Even less obvious movements of getting in and out of a stock car are made easier through increased flexibility. And if you experience lower back pain, it might simply be a result of tight hamstring muscles.

Strength training, when performed correctly, allows for freer body movement. It also leads to greater elasticity of soft tissues, most notably the muscles and tendons, and lessens the occurrence of spasms that can accompany stressful situations. You may question the benefits of flexibility for racing. Yet we're sure you will agree on its importance once you understand what "beneficial" flexibility really is.

To have flexible joints you must first have flexible muscles and connective tissue. And when a full or complete range of motion is present, your muscles become more capable of exerting greater force. Muscles that are limited in their range of motion (inflexible) tend to get injured and cramp more often. Cramping, however, in part may be a result of lacking minerals in your diet. (Chapter 3 explains this in more detail.)

The most important consideration when dealing with beneficial flexibility is not only the range of motion of a joint, but also the strength present in the extreme ranges of motion. This is what truly protects your joints from injury. Take, for example, a motocross racer who is rounding a corner. Not only is hip strength and flexibility needed to fully lean with the movement of the cycle, trunk and shoulder strength in a stretched position is needed too. Both measures aid in controlled balance in delicate situations like this. If flexibility is not present during this movement, you will either slow down, strain a "tight" muscle, or simply dump the bike and risk injury. And if your means of flexibility is through stretching alone, your risk of joint dislocation is elevated due to lacking beneficial flexibility.

If you have ever driven a car continuously for three or four hours, more often than not your lower back tightens up. It is common for tight hamstrings to be the culprit in this case. When tight, these muscles of your rear upper leg cause a pelvic tilt, resulting in lower back muscle strain. If hamstrings possess elastic qualities (flexibility), chances of this are reduced.

Just remember, to strengthen a joint in its extreme ranges of motion, you need complete range of motion exercise. And that's part of what proper strength training is all about. (Chapter 5 shows how this is done.)

2.2 Enhanced Coordination

Imagine yourself in the driver's seat of the Valvoline Ford Thunderbird NASCAR Winston Cup car. You're on the superspeedway at Talladega, driving at speeds approaching 200mph. You come upon lapped traffic that's going slower. Attempting to get through this traffic, your goal is to zoom in and out of cars, slowing only when brutally necessary. You check your rearview mirror to see if it is clear to go lower on the track as you near turn one. You go for it, slightly turning the wheel while you break momentarily, then hammering the accelerator. Well, fellow racing enthusiasts, it is eye-hand-foot coordination that makes this all happen.

Coordination is a learned trait. This is quite evident in early childhood when we learn to walk. But surprising to some, it is a trait that can be learned in our adult life too. Let's take a professional baseball player for example. Through proper training, eye-hand coordination improves, allowing a baseball player to connect a bat to a baseball thrown at 90mph.

Although eye-hand-foot coordination is something that is trained specifically—that is, with a specific stimulus and a specific reaction to the stimulus (such as driving a race car)—strength training can reduce the time it takes a muscle to contract after a message is sent to the muscle from the brain.

2.3 Improved Cardiovascular Efficiency

Although cardiovascular conditioning is best accomplished through more aerobic-type activities (such as cross-country skiing, walking, bicycling, and aerobic dancing), a strength training program set up in a nonstop circuit-type manner can produce similar results. For those who are not yet at a good fitness level, a strength training program can initially improve the effectiveness of your heart, lungs, and arteries (vessels that transport blood).

Properly performed strength training increases your heart's output (cardiac output) by lowering your heart rate at submaximal workloads (as in the case of racing) and at rest, and by increasing your heart's stroke volume (the amount of blood pumped at each heart contraction). In addition, such exercise forces you to breathe forcefully, consequently increasing the strength of your diaphragm muscles, making breathing less labored during intense physical activity. All of this makes for less racing fatigue, both physiologically and psychologically.

And as you may already know, physical fatigue often leads to mental fatigue.

If you normally tire before the end of the race, strength training will help to combat this early fatigue. Another side effect of such exercise is the enlargement of arteries, which reduces high blood pressure by permitting blood to flow easier. This is important to working muscles while they contract and during recovery from stressful situations, including exercise. In addition, it makes recovery from injury less time consuming.

2.4 Increasing Aerobic Power

Cardiovascular or aerobic conditioning pertains to the ability to engage in active physical activity for a sustained period of time, without becoming fatigued. For the most part, it involves your heart, arterial network (arteries and veins), lungs, and blood. It is the most important concern for health and fitness.

These four photos show the accident Mark Martin experienced at Talladega Superspeedway in 1991. When Mark's car began to get airborne he was traveling at a rate of at least 175mph. After the accident the car was repaired and Mark finished the race by driving another eighty-plus laps. The accident was scary, and the impact of the car coming in contact with the ground was ex- *tremely intense—you can see how high the car bounced after initially hitting the ground (second photo). If Mark had not had sufficient strength in his back and neck, chances are he would have injured his spine and been completely unable to control the car after it landed. This shows some of the paybacks of effective strength training.*

Through the elevation of heart and lung action observed during exercise, your cardiovascular-respiratory system becomes more efficient. That is, your heart pumps greater amounts of blood via a stronger heart contraction or beat (remember, it's a muscle) with less resistance to flow within the arteries and increases oxygen-carrying capabilities within the blood. The reason your cardiovascular system is so vital is that your heart pumps oxygen-filled blood throughout your body in order to maintain the function of each and every tissue. Oxygen

is needed by all bodily tissues to sustain life. And through inhaling, your lungs fill with oxygen that is in turn picked up by your blood and transported to the tissues. The gaseous waste products that result from the working muscles are then carried back to your lungs to be exhaled.

It has previously been believed that only sustained elevated heart rate exercise such as running and cycling would improve the efficiency of your cardiovascular system. However, a growing number of research studies has shown interval strength training to be a productive means of aerobic conditioning. Interval training raises your heart rate during intense work periods, then lowers it during passive periods. So your heart rate rises and then declines, rises and then declines, and so on. This can best be accomplished through circuit training. (Circuit training is explained in greater detail in Chapter 5.)

Of particular concern and yet seldom addressed is the matter involving the use of oxygen within the muscle cells. Even if your heart pumps oxygen-rich blood to the working muscles, the muscles will not efficiently use the oxygen unless they increase their levels of enzymes essential to oxygen utilization. Let's take running, for example. If the race driver and the pit crew spend their exercise time jogging, it's our belief that they may as well take a snooze. Even though the jogging will likely improve your overall health, the results are not specific to performance in racing. Rather, a strength training program designed with specific racing duties in mind can enhance heart and lung efficiency, along with muscle enzyme concentration needed for oxygen utilization within the exact muscles involved.

For you, the racer, aerobic endurance is important but should be improved upon in the activity that most resembles and benefits your performance on race day. And we strongly agree that strength training is *the* best means to overall condition yourself.

2.5 Strength Training for Endurance Racing

When your strength increases, so does your local muscle endurance and your strength endurance. Local muscle endurance refers to your ability to perform submaximal force output (muscle contractions) over a prolonged period of time. Strength endurance pertains to your ability to produce maximal force output time after time with little or no decline in strength.

This doesn't refer, however, to the maximal endurance required in events like running a marathon. But it does refer to the less-than-maximal endurance capacities of racing. For instance, even during a race lasting three to four hours, you are not performing at intense levels throughout the race. In fact, most races are more of an interval-type activity that finds you driving hard at some times and easy at others.

It's during the more passive situations that your body recovers somewhat from the intense, laborious driving. And the stronger and more fit you are, the quicker you'll recover in these situations.

To see how strength training increases your submaximal endurance, here's something you can do: Try lifting a brick above your head as many times as you can, then practice the same movement using a cinder block. Do this three times a week for six to eight weeks, then again lift the brick as many times as possible. The brick should feel so light that you are able to far surpass the number of times you initially lifted it. This is precisely how strength training increases muscular endurance.

Now you should have a better perception of how a stronger body can begin and continue throughout a race with less chances of early fatigue. These strength or endurance benefits may be more pronounced in oval track and road racing, in motocross, speedboat racing, and all-terrain vehicle endeavors. Yet the numerous repeat performance heats involved in drag racing require similar enduring strength for a reproduction of all-out, short-lived performance.

2.6 Lessened Injury Severity

Since it is established that stronger muscles, tendons, and bones require greater forces to cause them to break, tear, or strain, you can see how stronger tissues can be trained to withstand some of the outside forces experienced in racing. Although you cannot possibly prevent all injuries from occurring, it is possible to reduce the degree of injury you may receive. Keep in mind that this pertains not only to accidents on the racetrack; injury sometimes occurs in the pit lane, in the garage, and at home.

Because you can never predict or simulate an accident, you can best protect yourself from severe injury by stimulating your body to adapt to all facets of proper strength training.

Consider Mark Martin's accident in Talladega: If Mark had not had a strong back and neck, chances are he would have severely injured his spine when his car returned to the track with a severe jarring impact.

2.7 Recovery from Injury or Surgery

A truly beneficial effect that strength training has on the body is the ability to recover—both faster and better—from injury or surgery. One of the major reasons for this is the increase in blood flow to the muscles, tendons, ligaments, and bones. As your training program progresses, capillaries supplying blood to these tissues grow in size and number. Blood delivers nutrients essential to tissue rebuilding while removing unwanted waste material. Therefore, increased vascularization (blood supply) facilitated through strength training contributes to a shorter time for tissue repair.

Even during surgery, when muscles are surgically cut and then sutured (sewn back together), an increased capillary density allows more blood to reach the tissues, stimulating them to repair faster.

Interestingly, injury does not necessarily produce muscle weakness, especially when muscles are strong. Stronger muscles retain strength longer (than weaker muscles) when post-surgery immobilization is required. Furthermore, the improved nerve-muscle action facilitated by strength training contributes to quicker recovery by maintaining somewhat higher nerve activity within the muscle. And when a decline in neuromuscular activity is experienced through immobilization, a "reeducation" of coordination occurs faster in strength trained muscles.

Since strength training elevates your metabolism, your body becomes more effective in maintaining homeostasis (normal body functioning). This, in part, is a result of increased muscle tone and lean body mass (fat-free weight). And an elevated metabolism spurs a quicker turnover rate of injured tissue. Your body virtually repairs itself and thus recovers faster.

Increased abilities to recover from injury or surgery are not only reflective of strength training, but more so of your overall health. And although strength training can be a tool in achieving overall health, you should also concern yourself with vital matters of nutrition, rest, and stress. If in addition to regular exercise you follow good eating habits, get appropriate amounts of rest, and properly deal with stress, your body can literally concentrate on repairing itself. Otherwise, your body must deal with outside pressures that cause it to function in overdrive, and it therefore requires additional time for complete recovery.

2.8 Improving Heat Tolerance

Your body makes several adjustments in order for you, as a racer, to perform. Your body's ability to adapt and make adjustments is enhanced through strength training. Among these astonishing feats of adaptation is your body's ability to regulate its own temperature.

Although it is generally considered normal to have a body temperature of 98.6 degrees Fahrenheit, this value actually fluctuates within individuals. In an attempt to maintain a temperature that is normal for you, adjustments are made by your body, without your consent. For instance, in extreme heat, your body relies primarily on radiation and evaporation. Simply, your body's core radiates excess heat to your body's shell (skin), where it evaporates. And with excess cold, your body shivers. This generates a buildup of heat through increased metabolism, whereby maintaining your body's temperature.

Wind, humidity, and even your clothing influence your body's thermoregulation (ability to regulate heat). In a racing vehicle where temperatures can exceed 160 degrees while the driver wears a racing suit, unusually high temperatures reach the body. And most motorsports activities are performed during the hottest months of the year. In

effect, racing places the driver and sometimes the pit crew under severe heat conditions and subsequent risks of dehydration.

When you exercise or perform any other form of strenuous physical work in windy conditions, evaporation of sweat from your skin increases and a cooling effect occurs easily. When there is high humidity, your body has a more difficult time with evaporation and thus is harder to cool. In a dry environment where the air absorbs sweat at a faster rate, you may not even realize that you are sweating. Although exercise can be affected by these conditions, the only environmental factor affecting you as a race driver is the outside temperature. And as we said, it's usually hot.

When you strength train, your body temperature can be safely maintained at a level of 100 to 104 degrees Fahrenheit, providing cooling is made possible. It is important to know that when training with higher body temperatures, your body virtually becomes more efficient. This is one of the benefits of warmups. Through warming up, the viscosity of a muscle lessens, which enhances the force and speed of muscular contractions.

This might be better explained through the similar relationship of motor oil to a car. The more the oil heats up, the less viscous it becomes and the better it passes through the running engine.

So is the case with muscle. As you increase the temperature of your muscles, less friction is generated through your muscular movement. On a cellular level, a rise in muscle temperature produces accelerated metabolic reactions. This means that the accumulation of waste products resulting from muscular contractions will be delayed, preserving energy stores.

Among other valuable changes in the body, higher temperature within your muscles also improves nerve-muscle interaction and increases blood vessel size and, thus, blood flow. So you can see that increased body temperature can be advantageous during strength training. In racing, overheating your body is much more a risk than overheating your engine.

The longer you race or the longer you exercise, the greater your body builds up internal heat. This results in mental as well as physical stress. Also, the more intensely you drive or train, the more heat you build up. Although it is difficult to gradually increase your competitive racing intensity and duration, you can gradually increase these parameters of your strength training program. This will result in improved heat tolerance in the gym and in the race car.

When you sweat, you lose valuable water stores along with important minerals. And because much of the water comes from your blood, dangerous situations may arise due to your blood becoming too thick. This can slow the needed circulation of blood throughout your body and put a damper on your performance.

Rehydration through the consumption of water and diluted electrolyte solutions is vitally needed in cases of dehydration and potential dehydration. When you race and when you train, you should sip small amounts of water or sports drinks containing small amounts of carbohydrates (approximately a 7 percent concentration) and electrolytes. You need not wait until you are thirsty because your body can require additional fluids before you realize it through thirst. In fact, by the time you become thirsty, your body has already experienced some fluid losses.

Caution: Consuming large amounts of fluids at one time may produce stomach discomfort. Experience can help you determine how much is right for you.

A problem that everyone involved in the racing game should be aware of is heat stress. Although it is possible for an individual to tolerate heat of ninety degrees Fahrenheit and more, there is a limit at which benefits are outweighed by possible dangerous side effects. You don't need to have a heart condition to experience such dangerous effects. If your body becomes inefficient or unable to tolerate higher internal temperatures, you can experience such conditions as weakness, muscle cramping, nausea, loss of consciousness, and even death. For someone with any type of cardiovascular condition (such as arteriosclerosis), this is a more dangerous situation because that person is more susceptible to such problems.

You should realize that your body's ability to tolerate heat decreases with age. This is because many of the bodily functions responsible for regulating temperatures tend to be reduced as you age. Of course, the better physical condition you are in, the more tolerant you will be to heat buildup.

The accompanying table illustrates some of the most common heat-related problems encountered in racing. Notice how serious each can be. Remember, your best means of prevention is through frequent consumption of liquids.

The accompanying table illustrates the three major health problems associated with impaired thermoregulation of the body. Although proper exercise increases your body's tolerance to heat, a high risk is present in most forms of racing.

Although you should attempt to remain cool (physically) during racing endeavors, you should keep your body warm during strength training. This doesn't mean you allow your body to become overheated; it simply means that you need to break a sweat. Also, working out in a warm environment promotes the release of growth hormone. Growth hormone helps in building strength as well as losing body fat. Such a release is highly unlikely in cold or even cool workout rooms. So forget the air conditioning when you're training.

The way your body's thermoregulation system works depends on many factors. If your body becomes overheated, your work production will decrease and you will place your body in a potentially dangerous situation.

It is wise to remember that the best ways to train effectively in very warm environments, without thermoregulatory problems, is to do so at a level tolerable to your body. Simply, this means that you don't overdo it. Your training intensity and duration should be determined by your present-day physical condition. The better shape you are in,

Common Heat-Related Problems

Problem	Cause	Symptoms	Treatment
Muscle cramps	loss of body fluids and/or minerals	involuntary muscle contractions causing pain	stretch and attempt to relax muscle; massage may help; drink fluids containing electrolytes
Heat exhaustion	loss of blood due to lack of body fluids	cool, moist, gray skin, muscle cramps, confusion	if not sweating, wrap body in cool, wet towels; if sweating, consume cold liquids; regardless, get to hospital
Heat stroke	failure of the body's heat regulation system leading to build-up of heat inside the body	hot, dry skin, no sweat, muscle cramps, dizziness, weakness, headache, faint feelings and increased heart rate	as above; in need of immediate hospitalization

the more you can tolerate heat and the harder you can train for longer periods.

Training during early morning hours might prove beneficial in hot environments. And remember that your heat tolerance gradually reduces with age, so you may need to slow down a little over time. The accompanying chart describes some of the advantages and disadvantages of temperature (hot and cold) on body function. The effectiveness of your strength training can be influenced by the factors listed on the chart.

As the table indicates, your body adapts to changes in temperature in a positive or a negative manner. As a racing enthusiast as well as a strength trainer, you must know how to adjust in each situation.

Incidentally, if you have ever driven a race car in temperatures exceeding 90 degrees Fahrenheit, you know how it feels inside the car—where temperatures rise above 150 degrees. Any way that you can train your body to tolerate heat better is both an advantage and a safety mechanism.

Since strength training also increases the number of blood vessels feeding blood to various tissues (especially the muscles and skin), heat is more easily dissipated, making a heated race car (or boat, truck, or any enclosed cockpit) more tolerable for the driver.

2.9 Better Sleep

Science has demonstrated sleep improvement as a benefit of exercise, not only as a direct result of the acute physical activity (following a workout session), but also as a chronic effect of long-term training.

Sound sleep is something any racer or performance driving enthusiast needs in order to be at his or her best. In fact, athletes who are in good physical condition not only sleep more soundly, but are also more alert while awake. We're sure you know what could happen to someone who is not fully alert while driving 100-plus mph. It's quite obvious!

Research has compared those who exercise with those who don't. Sleep follows normal patterns in those who exercise. But non-exercisers sleep erratically and eventually develop chronic insomnia. Some even experience constipation.

There's no doubt that pounding the iron relaxes your body, making sleeping hours more beneficial. Although exercise increases your need for quality sleep, just as competition does, the amount

---

Effects of Temperature in Racing and Strength Training

Factor	Potential Dangers	Potential Benefits
Hot environment	May cause heat stress	Keeps you warmed up
Cold environment	May be responsible for muscle tears and strains	Allows for additional cooling
Plastic sweats	Do not allow for evaporation and can cause heat stress	None
Magnitude of heat	The higher it is, the more your body works to keep cool	The lower it is, the more your body works to maintain a normal level
Humidity	The greater it is, the harder it is to keep cool in heated environments, and the harder it is to keep warm in cool environments	None
Exercise duration	The longer you train, the harder it is to keep cool in heated environments and the harder it is to keep warm in cool environments	Increases as you get in better physical condition
Acclimatization	Changing to different environments will reduce your physical performance	By training in heated and cool environments, your body will improve its ability to tolerate various temperatures

of sleep you actually need is an individual matter. In most cases, six to eight hours a night suffices.

To a road rally racer who drives for hours on end, sleep deprivation leads to poor performance due to lack of concentration and subsequent low driving intensity. However, in the short bursts of intense concentration involved in events such as drag racing, the lack of sleep will be less profound. Still, the cumulative effect of several days of sleep loss can lead to slower eye-foot coordination at the green light.

If you go sleepless for even one night, your abilities to remain alert start to diminish. Strength training improves your ability to sleep more soundly. In fact, most athletes claim they don't sleep as well during layoffs from exercise training.

Feeling tired during the day can dramatically affect your racing performance. But a short catnap can help. It has been shown that a short period of sleep during the day relaxes you and significantly reduces feelings of stress. But remember to nap for no more than twenty to forty-five minutes. Longer amounts can take you into a deep sleep, which will leave you feeling drowsy.

2.10 Improved Alertness

Research has shown that strength training can increase alertness. You don't have to be an Einstein to realize the importance of this effect. With speeds constantly increasing along with a concomitant increased risk of injury, being alert can help you become a winner, and possibly save your life.

By increasing storage capabilities of energy within the muscles and liver as a result of vigorously exercising your muscles, it takes more physical and mental stress to hamper your performance. In fact this, together with improved sleep patterns and stress control, helps to maintain higher energy levels with a subsequent greater concentration level as well.

2.11 Dealing with Stress

Stress—something we all experience, something some of us thrive on. Without it, most of us would not perform our best. But too much stress can get you down. When used properly, stress forces you to do the best you can, to try harder than you are accustomed to.

But in the realm of motorsports racing, with personality traits similar for almost all drivers (high levels of anxiety and aggression), stress is likely to be a negative factor affecting performance on the racetrack. And for those experiencing off-track stress, strength training can be a means of venting frustration and anger—all while you are getting into better physical condition.

Think about it: Exercise not only benefits your body, it can help your mind as well. Several research studies have shown a direct relationship of physical fitness, mental alertness, and emotional stability.

Studies at the United States Military Academy at West Point reinforced this contention when researchers compared initial physical aptitude test scores with attrition rates. Those who scored higher had a 50 percent lower attrition rate than those scoring low. In addition, those with higher scores performed better in physical training as well as in classroom studies.

Beneficial reductions in anger and increases in "controlled" anxiety are often experienced through a strengthening exercise program. In addition, feelings of well-being are improved, thus helping to control behavior. Basically, it allows the racer facing difficult situations to keep his or her "cool."

Removing yourself from stressful situations is not always possible. In the high-pressure world of racing, stress is common. Stresses related to racing and other outside concerns have a profound impact on your racing readiness. A stress response can take a deathly toll on your energy levels, recovery from injury and illness, and race performance.

Here's how stress works within your body: Your brain sends messages throughout your body to create readiness, a response to stress that prepares you for action—the well-known "fight or flight" syndrome. This causes your heart to beat faster so your body has more available energy while oxygen-filled blood circulates more to your muscles. As all of this transpires, your senses of eyesight and smell sharpen due to associated nerve stimulation. Your adrenal gland pumps adrenaline throughout your body and causes an elevation of blood-sugar for quick energy. Air passages dilate, allowing for deeper breathing.

As you can see, outside stresses that you experience can either drain your body of energy or gear you up for performance. And no matter what kind of shape you're in, failure to properly deal with stress can result in a far less than optimal performance. In fact, it can cause you to prematurely reach the end of your racing career.

But by taking advantage of a release from stress through strength training, you become more capable of venting frustrations, increase your self-confidence and self-accomplishment, and subsequently can better cope with the pitfalls of racing.

Having high levels of stress for prolonged periods has a detrimental effect on your body. It can produce chronic bouts of diarrhea, constipation, weakness, sleep deprivation, and muscle spasms. And we needn't tell you the effects any of these have on racing.

As we all know too well, stress affects us mentally too, leading to the likes of depression, impatience, and irritability, as well as an inability to concentrate, relax, think clearly, or cope. Good luck trying to compete with any one of these problems without strength training!

High levels of acute (severe, short-term) stress can also affect your health. It can increase your cholesterol, lead to high blood pressure, produce nausea, heartburn, and eyestrain, facilitate tightness in the muscles of your jaw and neck, reduce smooth coordinated movements, and give you a headache. In general, stress can affect your overall health in a way that impairs your performance.

Strength training obviously has a favorable effect on the way you look. Your attitude about yourself improves and you become happier with what you have done to your body. This often results in greater self-satisfaction, sense of achievement and well-being, and personal effectiveness. As a result, you feel more confident in everything you do. This is not just theory. We have seen this change in literally hundreds of individuals.

In this sense, strength training serves as a therapeutic tool for emotional release. It's a form of preventative medicine, virtually helping you deal with stress so it doesn't increase your chances of disease, illness, and injury. It permits you to channel your aggression to work for you—in smart exercise and racing. To have something other than driving on your mind while driving nearly 200mph is called suicide. Total concentration on what you are doing is not only a recommendation for successful racing, it is a necessity for survival.

2.12 Overall Health Benefits

A healthy driver is one who can compete in absence of illness or disease. And there's no way you can perform well if you don't feel well. To be healthy during an entire racing season requires you to take good care of your body. The adage, if you don't use it you lose it, reflects the various functions of your body. And to sit behind a powerful motor when you are ill is, at best, pretty stupid. Remember, not only is *your* life on the line, but also those of your competitors.

In addition to the benefits already mentioned, we must not neglect a major benefit of healthy living: improved overall health. Sure, strength training protects you against injury, helps you to deal with stress, and improves general function of the body. Even more importantly, it helps you maintain a healthy body, whether you're a racer or not.

It is questionable whether or not exercise actually adds years to your life, although an increasing number of studies indicate such a possibility. However, it is well established that it adds quality to your life. This alone can provide you with additional years of racing competition or performance driving.

To have an effective immune system is crucial to warding off illness and disease. Living in our toxic environment coupled with the ever-increasing consumption of preservatives in our foods makes us all age more quickly. And this can mean a deterioration of physiological function and ability to fight off disease, illness, and sometimes subsequent injury. Some of these diseases and illnesses can be prevented. Through regular participation in a strength training regime, your immune system becomes more effective. Interestingly, though, athletes who reduce their body fat to extremely low levels while exercising excessively virtually lower the effectiveness of their immune system. It is unlikely, however, that anyone involved in racing has this much time to exercise. And providing a proper diet is followed, chances of an impaired immune system are remote.

It is also possible for strength training to reduce the levels of LDL-cholesterol (low-density lipoproteins—the bad guys) and total cholesterol, along with increasing HDL-cholesterol (high density lipoproteins—the good guys). This helps to protect you from heart disease.

The latter, HDL, helps to reduce plaque buildup on the walls of your arteries. Because the buildup of plaque in the arteries (arteriosclerosis) is known as a silent killer, these improvements in health may only be known through a blood test, not actually "felt." But an end product of arteriosclerosis is poor blood flow throughout your body and a subsequent risk of heart attack and stroke. When blood flow is restricted, muscles tire more quickly, which you certainly don't want to happen while driving.

Lowering your high blood pressure (hypertension) is another side effect of such regular exercise. Interestingly, it's not only aerobic exercise that produces these effects. An increasing amount of research is supporting strength training as a factor in getting more favorable blood pressure levels.

And since strength training can improve the body's sensitivity to insulin, such exercise can be a valuable means of prevention and treatment for some forms of diabetes. This, together with changes noted in cholesterol and blood pressure regulation, can significantly lower your risk for some forms of cancer as well as heart disease.

Strength training can also improve the effectiveness of the digestive system by acting as a natural cathartic—an agent that promotes defecation by increasing bowel movement and reducing the risk and discomfort of being bloated and constipated during races. In fact, a recent article appearing in *Medicine and Science in Sports and Exercise* (Vol. 24, No. 4) has shown such an increase in bowel transit time, as a result of strength training, to reduce the risks of colon cancer in men.

In conclusion, many side effects of proper strength training can be beneficial to any motorsports participant. Such physical training should be a requirement, not an option for all who take part in this game of speed and skill.

2.13 Physical Benefits Lead to Mental Benefits

We have seen that through regular physical exercise, the body improves its ability to ward off illnesses and disease. Numerous medical studies have proven that these effects stimulate a more functional immune system. And surprising to some ill-advised individuals, strength training is among the forms of exercise that can produce these benefits.

But precautionary measures are needed. If you are a fanatic and strength train carelessly, without allowing your body to fully recuperate from previous workouts, you can impair your immune system, thereby placing yourself at higher risk for illness, disease, and injury. (Chapter 5 discusses this in detail.)

To have a healthy mind as well as a healthy body is crucial to success in any venture. You can be physically fit, but drowning from mental stress. Body and mind can work together beneficially, or they can place limitations on each other. But there should be no doubt, you need to be physically and mentally refreshed on race day and during practice in order to race to your potential.

Through strength training, your body is gradually molded—literally—into better shape. You soon will see that all the hard work has produced not only a more functional body, but also one that is visually improved. The knowledge that you are stronger and more physically fit will improve your sense of well-being, which can translate to self-confidence and which, in turn, leads to controlled aggression. Although aggressive behavior is a requisite of racing, your ability to channel aggression into performance becomes more effective. You're able to think faster and more confidently about what you are doing.

As you may already know, people who are in poor physical condition are often embarrassed about themselves and can lack confidence. They don't feel good about themselves or what they do. The result is that they don't perform well. But with a drive to improve the way you look and feel, an entire attitude adjustment occurs. The stronger, more fit person looks better, feels better, and performs better. Just think of the impact this alone has on racing!

2.14 Driving for Racing

Obviously, strength training should be mandatory for every race driver and pit crew member, whether they consider themselves athletes or not. We consider each person involved in racing as an athlete. It's a physically and mentally demanding activity that can be improved upon through proper physical training, just like any other competitive endeavor.

If every team member is in top physical shape, then the performance of the race vehicle and the success of the race strategy are the main variables separating winners from losers. Strength training helps you eliminate weak links in the chain leading to success.

And more importantly, you have a means of increasing bodily protection from injury, illness, and possible death. This is the greatest lasting benefit of all.

Chapter 3

Importance of Diet

When you're active, your body depends on protein for growth and carbohydrates for fuel. To benefit from your exercise and succeed in your motorsports endeavors, you must remember: you're only as good as your diet.

When you're active, your body depends on protein for growth and carbohydrates for fuel. To achieve beneficial results from your exercise and success in your driving endeavors, you must remember— you're only as good as your diet.

This chapter discusses smart eating made simple. Although nutritional concerns can be very complicated, we have elected to bypass the chemical relationships of various foodstuffs and get to the nitty-gritty.

We have listed seven reasons why a racer should maintain a nutritionally balanced diet. Each reason's description presents specific guidelines, for which some adjustments in eating habits may be necessary.

3.1 Overall Health

Whether you exercise intensely or you simply perform laborious racing duties, you can damage your body if you do not maintain a nutritious diet.

Your body needs nutrients in order to function normally. This is crucial for the constant rebuilding of cells that occurs inside your body as well as to supply energy for normal functioning of your brain, heart, muscles, and bones, among other vital organs. And as you stress your body, physically and mentally, your demand for nutrition increases to meet the ever-demanding need to combat fatigue and weakness.

For instance, certain foods can help increase the effectiveness of your immune system. In fact, some even ward off certain diseases and illnesses, including selected forms of cancer and heart disease.

Surprising to most people, exercise and the performance of vigorous duties on the racetrack cause the release of chemical substances that often damage proteins and other cells. These chemicals, known as free-radicals, can cause a series of reactions that in turn cause destruction of body cells. Such cell destruction can lead to numerous health problems, including insufficient tissue rebuilding.

However, foods high in vitamins C and E can help in defending you against the buildup of these radicals. These vitamins, together with a form of vitamin A known as beta-carotene, are collectively referred to as antioxidants and fight against these free-radicals. This is only one of several ways your diet affects your health.

By becoming deficient in any vitamins or minerals, you can place yourself at risk for illness and disease. For example: Vitamin C has been linked with the release of opiate-like brain chemicals called endorphins. These chemicals are also referred to as stress-altering substances that help to produce a restorative effect on your body and help you stay healthy.

What you eat, how often you eat, and how much you eat determine the nutritional support your body receives—or doesn't receive.

3.2 Energy Enhancement

In many racing events, quick, intense bursts of energy are required for best performance. This can be referred to as "quick energy." And any means to promote a quicker rebuilding of energy for muscle contractions will be beneficial.

To provide your muscles with a quick energy source, sugar must be stored inside your muscle cells in the form of muscle glycogen and in your blood as glucose. By consuming certain types of carbohydrate foods, you will spare your muscle glycogen and be more capable of performing at higher intensities for longer periods without becoming fatigued. This will be discussed in greater detail later in the chapter.

When you race for more than one hour (as in NASCAR's Winston Cup racing) or repeat your performance during several heats of racing (as in drag racing), you need similar long-duration energy supplies in order to be effective and successful. This not only increases your requirements for energy-producing foods, it also increases your need for various minerals often referred to as electrolytes. These minerals influence various bodily functions, including muscle contraction and relaxation.

For a better understanding of how you need to eat, first you need to understand how your energy-producing system works. When you perform low-intensity work, fuel for muscular contraction comes from the sugar in your blood. But when you increase your work intensity, more of the energy comes from the sugar stored within your working muscles (glycogen). This energy source is short-lived and must be replenished by those sugars stored within your liver and circulating in your blood. Failure to provide your body with energy-producing food leads to early fatigue.

3.3 Increasing Strength and Muscle Size

Strength is another reason racers need to eat. Strength is of unquestionable significance in your racing performance. As the old adage goes, only the strong will survive. This is *so* true in racing!

Inadequate consumption of foods containing protein and carbohydrates will leave your racing and strength training at a standstill—with no appreciable benefits. In fact, you'll feel fatigued and weak while racing, something we're sure you don't want to experience.

Since protein aids in muscle growth, and larger muscles are usually stronger muscles, protein plays an important role in strength improvement. And because carbohydrates provide energy for muscular work and are stored within your muscles, liver, and blood, carbohydrates are equally as important in building stronger muscles. These two nutritional concerns contribute heavily to the stimulation of full recuperation from exercise, stress, injury, illness, and rigorous racing duties. And without full recovery, strength and muscle size will not improve.

3.4 Fat Loss

In an effort to minimize the weight your vehicle must carry around during a race, you should have a lean body—with little in the way of body fat. But you must remember one important factor when considering fat loss: You still need to *eat* while losing weight. No crash diets!

Your goal should be to lose excess weight (fat) while maintaining or increasing the weight of your muscle tissue and bones. Your body still has an essential need for nutrients necessary for tissue growth, repair, and function. And with the combined effects of strength training and racing, your nutritional needs elevate.

It's all in the way you eat and what you eat. We'll go into more detail on this later in the chapter.

3.5 Improved Mental Concentration

Aside from low levels of physical activity associated with low levels of energy, insufficient carbohydrate consumption can leave you without the capability to concentrate on anything you do. To any racer, this can be disastrous.

If you have ever limited your food intake severely, you most likely noticed feelings of weakness, fatigue, and lethargy. It eventually became difficult to stay awake. In addition, your ability to think clearly and make reasonable decisions was restricted. Whether you knew it or not, your entire thought process was and always is affected by your nutrition.

Eating properly is the answer to both good physical and mental performance. A diet that provides ample carbohydrates provides you with the necessary energy sources needed by your brain, heart, and muscles. If you limit this source of energy, these vital organs will not work to their capacities.

3.6 Recovery from Exercise

To fully recover from the stresses associated with strength training, nutritional demands are boosted. Kart racers as well as elite Indy car racers should attempt to train intensely in order to perform better in their respective forms of racing. This more intense training requires a bigger rebuilding process, in which protein as well as carbohydrates are crucial agents.

Improper nutritional practices can leave you weak, sore, and unproductive. The significance of a well-balanced diet is unquestionable. The fact that hard-working (mentally and physically) individuals require additional nutritional support is equally unquestionable.

One requirement for anyone training hard is the consumption of quality protein. Research has shown us time and time again that protein requirements increase as a result of demanding physical exercise. But not only does the body require additional protein for the rebuilding of muscle tissue, requirements for carbohydrates also can increase simultaneously. As your muscles work intensely, they burn energy stored within the muscles (glycogen). Science tells us that these energy stores must be refilled completely in order to again perform maximal work. To do this, you need a diet that is high in complex carbohydrates.

When you strength train, you sweat away some valuable vitamins and minerals. As a result of this happening day after day, in absence of full replenishment, conditions such as dehydration can take place. When that occurs, it takes a longer time to fully recover.

3.7 Recovery from Injury, Illness, and Disease

When you are ill or injured, certain foodstuffs help you to get better. Carbohydrates can help give you the energy needed to maintain general function of vital organs like your brain and heart. Fats will help by serving as a carrier for the fat-soluble vitamins. Protein aids by influencing your immune system, thereby protecting against infection while increasing the speed of healing.

As a matter of fact, protein contributes greatly to many processes that take place inside your body. And a deficiency in any of the amino acids (building blocks of protein) can mean it will take a longer time before full recovery.

Even a deficiency of some vitamins can lead to longer recovery times. For instance, vitamin C (ascorbic acid) is crucial for fighting fatigue and stress that often cause and can be a result of sickness and injury. A lack of this vitamin consequently hinders recovery from injury and illness.

3.8 When to Eat

Now that you have a better understanding of *why* good nutrition is necessary for racing, you can learn how to be smart about your eating. It is equally important to know when to eat. The chief reasons that you cannot eat randomly are:
- For sufficient energy to perform the work in and on your race vehicle
- For training recuperation
- For additional filling of stores essential for greater workloads
- For body weight maintenance or increases or losses, and
- To ensure proper bodily functions. Remember, as a vigorously working motorsports enthusiast, your needs are different from those of the average individual.

Scientific research shows that you can burn nearly one-third more calories during stresses accompanying pre-race nervousness. Even the caloric expenditure during a race can be higher than that utilized during strength training sessions.

It is a well-established fact that diet allows you to be more active and perform better as a rac-er. Your diet needs to meet both your energy demands and nutritional substance requirements. However, your diet will be effective only when it meets all of the various demands placed on it through exercise and racing.

Smart eating is the means by which you fit your nutrition to your exercise and racing. This can best be done through the consumption of five meals a day, rather than the more conservative approach of three a day.

A major concern you should have as an active individual—during your strength training, in the garage, on race day, or at leisure—is your blood-sugar level. Following a meal, your blood-sugar is elevated. This allows you to perform physical activity without energy loss. Of course, the more laborious your activity, the more you reduce these levels. And when your blood-sugar level gets low, you will feel tired and weak.

By learning to "listen to your body," you will be inclined to realize when your blood-sugar is low and replenishment is needed. This is the time to eat again. That is why we strongly recommend a meal every three to four hours.

Rather than eating by the clock or when you are hungry, you should attempt to consume all five to six daily meals in a 15-18-hour period. This is the time you are usually awake. It is advised, however, that you not eat within two hours of going to sleep. Since your metabolism slows during sleep, it is likely that at least some of the calories consumed will be stored as fat. If it is absolutely necessary that you eat before retiring, consume a meal higher in protein than carbohydrates. A high-carbohydrate meal may impair your ability to sleep soundly.

Ideally, although not always practically, you should eat more before your most active periods. Say for instance you are preparing for a big race tomorrow. Your last meal today should be high in carbohydrates. This is an attempt to refill any and all energy stores in your muscles and liver. The meal prior to the race, which should be eaten about two to three hours before suiting up, should also be almost entirely complex carbohydrates. This helps to maintain energy levels during the race.

3.9 What to Eat

As any exercise physiologist or nutritional expert will agree, driving skill and adequate strength are just not enough to obtain a competitive edge. Proper nutrition also contributes immensely to your peak performance.

Six major nutrients are necessary for a healthy, strong body. These are: carbohydrates, proteins, fats, vitamins, minerals, and water. Remember, to anyone involved in the racing game, a deficiency in any one of these nutrients can reduce your chances of success.

Carbohydrates

Every driver, everyone on the pit crews, and every mechanic all have one similar requirement: the need for energy. And the best source of energy comes from carbohydrates. Ultimately, 50-80 percent of your caloric intake should consist of carbohydrates. But let's not complicate this by using measurements (calories). We'll simply state that the greatest share of every meal, with the exception of eating right before bedtime, should be made up of carbohydrates.

Carbohydrates can be classified in three ways: monosaccharides, disaccharides, and polysaccharides. Simple sugars like glucose and fructose fall into the monosaccharide category. These simple sugars can be found in honey and fruits. Disaccharides are sugars like table sugar (sucrose) and lactose. Lactose is a sugar found in milk.

The third class, or polysaccharides, are those sugars often referred to as complex carbohydrates. These sugars are starches (dextrins, cellulose, pectin, and glycogen) that can be found in whole grains, vegetables, nuts, some fruits and legumes.

When you consume carbohydrates, your digestive system converts them to blood-sugar (glucose). As previously mentioned, this glucose is stored in your muscle cells and in your liver as glycogen. Glucose in your blood provides energy for brain function.

When you perform intense work, glycogen stored within your muscles provides most of the energy for muscular contractions. When your intensity is low to moderate, your blood-sugar acts as an energy source.

If there is leftover glucose in your blood following a refilling of carbohydrate stores, the remaining carbohydrates are stored as fat. This is in part why you shouldn't gorge yourself during any one meal—there's almost always leftover blood-sugar.

By consuming a food with a low glycemic index rating, you will experience a more stabilized blood-sugar level. The Glycemic Index is a handy rating system that tells you what carbohydrates provide the best energy for prolonged periods. The lower the rating, the more sustained the energy source within the blood. The accompanying table illustrates the ratings of selected food types. Remember, the lower the assigned number, the longer the carbohydrate takes to break down into blood-sugar and subsequently the longer you will have available energy within your blood.

Caution: Although fructose has a low rating, meaning that it is metabolized slowly, a large intake of any sugar, fructose included, is *not* recommended because it can cause a rise in triglyceride production. And high triglyceride levels for long periods have been linked with increased risk for coronary heart disease.

Each meal should be comprised mainly of carbohydrates, especially of the complex type. And obviously, the more active you are going to be, the more carbohydrates you will need. That means before your workouts and before the race.

Protein

Contrary to what some nutritionists believe, athletes *do* need more protein when they are training. It is estimated that athletes require anywhere from 0.42 to 1.0 grams of protein per pound of body weight per day. This is far and above that required by inactive individuals, which, incidentally, is the basis from which the National Research Council's Recommended Daily Allowances (RDA) has been established. In fact you would have to be an outright fool to think that hard-working individuals have the same protein requirements as sedentary ones.

Glycemic Index Rating of Foods

90-100
Carrots
Glucose
Parsnips

80-90
Corn Flakes
Honey
Potatoes (instant)

70-79
Bread (whole wheat)
Broad beans
Dates
Millet
Rice (white)
Watermelon
White potato

60-69
Bananas
Beets
Bread (white)
Mars Bar
Raisins
Rice (brown)
Shredded Wheat
Swiss Muesli
Water biscuits

50-59
All-Bran
Oatmeal biscuits
Pastries
Peas (frozen)
Potato chips
Spaghetti (white)
Sucrose
Sweet corn
Yams

40-49
Buckwheat pancakes
Dried peas

Grapes
Navy beans
Oatmeal
Orange juice
Oranges
Porridge oats
Spaghetti (whole
 wheat)
Sponge cakes
Sweet potato
Whole grain rye
 bread

30-39
Apples
Blackeye peas
Butter beans
Chick peas
Fish sticks
Green beans
Ice cream
Lima beans
Pears
Skim milk
Tomato soup
Whole milk
Yogurt

20-29
Barley
Cherries
Fructose
Grapefruit
Kidney beans
Lentils
Peaches
Plums
Sausages

10-19
Peanuts
Soybeans

Protein makes up nearly half of the dry weight of your body. It has been discovered that within six months, all protein is broken down and completely rebuilt. And although some protein aids in the repair and growth of your hair, skin, nails, muscles, and brain, some is lost through natural excretion processes—in the urine and the feces.

During intense, heavy exercise, blood cells are destroyed. When this occurs, protein is used to rebuild the cells. Even when you sweat, some proteins are lost. Whatever the reason, it is vital to know that additional protein is needed in proportion to your body's demand for it. The more intense your strength training, the more protein is required for repair and growth.

When you consume protein, it is broken down into the "building blocks of protein" commonly referred to as amino acids. There are twenty-two amino acids that are constructed in a certain pattern to make human protein. Of these twenty-two, twelve are usually found in sufficient quantities. Your body can actually manufacture these proteins.

The other ten building blocks are "essential," or those that are not manufactured by your body. They must be obtained through your diet. When a deficiency is found in any of these essential amino acids, the repair and rebuilding processes become less effective.

To complicate this further, although you may obtain sufficient quantities of protein in your diet, the structure of the amino acids may not be optimal. In essence, the protein source is critical to ensuring the intake of all of the essential amino acids.

For this reason, protein is rated by means of the protein efficiency ratio (PER). The PER of protein basically reflects its quality. While some foods can be classified as incomplete proteins (for example, all fruits and most vegetables), others include all the essential amino acids and are regarded as complete proteins (eggs and milk, for instance). Egg protein like that found in an egg white contains all the essential amino acids in proper proportions and has the highest PER available. Therefore, egg protein is the most highly assimilated or utilized of all types of protein. It is possible, but sometimes difficult, to combine foods in a way that all essential amino acids are provided. This sometimes poses a problem for vegetarians.

A protein deficiency can result in growth abnormalities and interferes with proper tissue development. If you lack protein in your diet, you can expect to have less energy, be tired, weak, and mentally depressed, have a lowered resistance to infections and disease, experience slower healing of injuries, and take longer to recover from exercise.

On the other hand, consuming more protein than your body can utilize also presents a problem. Your liver virtually converts the excess protein into fat, which is stored in your body—often at the waistline. And yet another problem can arise with overconsumption of protein. An extremely high intake of protein for a prolonged period can lead to the formation of a highly toxic ammonia called urea. Since your body excretes urea, an overabundance of the substance places a strain on your liver and kidneys and often times is responsible for causing a form of arthritis known as gout.

The timing for protein consumption is just as important as the quality. When you exercise, your body actually decreases its protein production. This can last for hours following your training at which time a rebuilding phase begins. This is an important time to consume high-quality protein. However, it is not just during this time that protein should be consumed. In fact, nearly every meal should include a quality protein source in order to allow your body to utilize the amino acids, when it needs them.

As your strength training and laborious racing duties increase in volume, duration, or intensity, your protein requirements increase accordingly. And with the increased need for quality protein, you should consume foods that have a high protein efficiency ratio. Recommended foods are egg whites, low-fat milk, lean meat, poultry, and fish.

The accompanying chart provides a valid way to estimate your daily protein requirements. The formula was developed by Fred Hatfield, Ph.D., director of the International Sports Sciences Association, in an effort to help athletes *and* non-athletes determine how much protein they should consume.

Keep in mind that your fat cells do not require protein. So it is necessary to determine your protein requirements based on your fat-free weight, also called your lean body weight. This is most accurately measured by means of underwater weighing techniques. However, a less expensive and nearly as accurate method is skinfold measurement. This measurement must be determined by a qualified sports fitness expert in order to be valid. Various body-part measurements (anthropometric measurement) can be made to predict body-fat percentages. But the validity of such measurement is questionable. Another technique known as electrical impedance utilizes small electrical current sent through your body to determine electrical conductance. The accuracy of this technique, however, is still controversial at the present time.

It is likely that if you perform physical racing duties throughout the week and on race day, along with strength training three times a week, you will need between 0.7 and 0.9 grams of protein per pound of lean body weight. For a 150lb person who has 15 percent body fat, this calculates to roughly

90 to 115 grams of protein daily—quite a bit more than the RDA, which calculates to about 63 grams per day.

Fats

As a racing enthusiast, you should realize the importance of fat in your diet. Fat is not always the culprit responsible for clogging your arteries and adding inches to your waistline. Rather, fat acts as a secondary source of energy during training or competition. Fat-based energy becomes available soon after carbohydrate stores within your muscles (glycogen) are depleted.

But first you need to understand what fats really are. Often referred to as lipids, fats can be found in solid or liquid form. And even though carbohydrates are your body's major source of energy, fats are the most highly concentrated source of energy over carbohydrates and proteins. Fats have nine calories per gram, while carbohydrates and proteins contain only four. Now you see why foods high in fat are also high in calories.

There are a host of reasons why your body needs fats. Fats act as the storage substance for excess calories that you consume. This applies not only to fats, but also to excess carbohydrates and proteins, although this seldom should be the case. Fat is an essential ingredient in maintaining healthy skin and hair, in addition to acting as a carrying agent in the transporting of the fat-soluble vitamins A, D, E, and K. Fats in your diet provide you with essential fatty acids, which are those the body does not manufacture. These essential fatty acids aid many bodily functions, including the regulation of blood pressure and the regulation of cholesterol in your blood. In addition, fats provide satiety (a sense of fullness) because they increase the time needed to empty food from your stomach.

What you need to be concerned with is what kinds of and how much fat should be in your daily diet. All fats are found as numerous combinations of saturated and unsaturated fatty acids. Fats that are of a high saturation usually come from animal sources like meat, milk, and butter. Exceptions are coconut and palm oils. These are vegetable oils, which are also highly saturated. With the exception of these two vegetable oils, saturated fats usually remain solid at room temperature.

Unsaturated fats are often classified as either monounsaturated fats (olive, peanut, and avocado oils) or polyunsaturated fats (corn, sesame, and safflower oils). The major concern for unsaturated fats is that they are of plant and fish origin. These fats usually remain liquid at room temperature and remain usable for only a short period.

To complicate things more, there is a process called hydrogenation, which makes unsaturated fats more saturated. This process is done to preserve the shelf life of unsaturated fats. No better for you than saturated fats, hydrogenated unsaturated fats become solid. Such is the case with most margarines and shortenings that remain solid at room temperature.

Although many health risks are associated with a high intake of saturated fat, *any* type of fat, whether it's saturated or unsaturated, can add inches to your waistline. Remember, one gram of any fat has nine calories. And since fat contains such a high number of calories, a high consumption of fat can easily lead to obesity. This increases your chances of heart disease and reduces your chances of a healthy, strong body.

A primary concern to everyone is cholesterol,

Hatfield Estimate Procedure for Determining Daily Protein Requirements

Formula: Lean Body Weight (in pounds) x Need Factor = Daily Protein Requirements (in grams)

Need factors:
0.5: Sedentary, no sports or training
0.6: Jogger or light fitness training
0.7: Sports participation or moderate training three times a week
0.8: Moderate daily weight training or aerobic training
0.9: Heavy weight training daily
1.0: Heavy weight training daily plus sports training, or twice-a-day training

Lean Body Wt (lb)	Need Factor (Protein requirements in grams per day)					
	0.5	0.6	0.7	0.8	0.9	1.0
90	45	54	63	72	81	90
100	50	60	70	80	90	100
110	55	66	77	88	99	110
120	60	72	84	96	108	120
130	65	78	91	104	117	130
140	70	84	98	112	126	140
150	75	90	105	120	135	150
160	80	96	112	128	144	160
170	85	102	119	136	153	170
180	90	108	126	144	162	180
190	95	114	133	152	171	190
200	100	120	140	160	180	200
210	105	126	147	168	189	210
220	110	132	154	176	198	220
230	115	138	161	184	207	230
240	120	144	168	192	216	240

Source: Complete Guide to Fitness Training, International Sports Sciences Association (ISSA), 1991. Used with permission from Fred Hatfield, Ph.D., Director.

another fat that is associated with fats in your diet. Known as the "silent killer," arteriosclerosis or plaque buildup in the arteries is a result of a high concentration of cholesterol in your blood. Although cholesterol is manufactured by your body, it is a useful agent in cell membrane and nerve fiber construction and acts in the building of some hormones.

A problem occurs, however, when the cholesterol that is circulating in your blood sticks to the walls of your arteries. This closes off blood flow and can lead to a heart attack or stroke.

Cholesterol is found in foods that come from animal sources like meats and dairy products. Both of these food types are high in saturated fats unless, of course, they are labeled no-fat. Be cautious of foods advertised as "no cholesterol." Although they may not contain cholesterol, they may contain cholesterol-producing saturated fat. *Read the labels!*

Cholesterol in your body is usually processed by your liver. Exceptions to this include: when certain diseases are present; when too much cholesterol or saturated fat is consumed; or when a sedentary lifestyle causes muscle wasting (atrophy) to take place. Although your body produces less cholesterol if you are consuming high levels of cholesterol or saturated fat, it's neither healthy nor desirable for you to consume too much of either one. Yet the amount of cholesterol your body itself produces is highly infuenced by heredity.

As noted earlier in the book, two main forms of cholesterol exist in your body. One is low-density cholesterol, often referred to as LDL (low-density lipoproteins because of its combination of fats with proteins). This carries the cholesterol through the bloodstream to deposit it for cell building. A problem that arises is that the excess LDL becomes attached to the artery walls, closing off the arterial opening.

High-density cholesterol (HDL) attaches to these excess LDL cholesterol deposits and takes them to the liver for remanufacturing or excretion. For these reasons alone, LDL is labeled as "bad" cholesterol and HDL as "good" cholesterol.

Since saturated fats usually stimulate the production of LDL, a high consumption of saturated fats will raise your overall cholesterol levels and increase your risk of heart disease. But what is important for you to know is that polyunsaturated fats can *lower* your levels of LDL. Recent research shows that some polyunsaturated fats found in fish oil might even provide additional benefits. The oil reduces the chances of blood clotting, thereby lowering your chances of blocked arteries. In addition, monounsaturated oils like olive oil recently have been found to contain LDL-lowering properties.

Although some nutritionists preach that fats make up 10-15 percent of your total daily caloric intake, the whole idea of calorie counting becomes more complicated when calculations are required. We recommend an intake of 10-15 grams of fat per day for those weighing under 200lb, and 20-25 grams for those weighing more than 200. Most of this fat should be unsaturated in nature. Consuming less can stimulate your body to produce extra cholesterol, thereby raising your cholesterol levels.

Vitamins

Everyone needs vitamins. People who exercise and perform strenuous duties in their occupations or during leisure time need more vitamins than most other people. If you want to be a successful racer, you must provide your body with everything it needs. Vitamins are undoubtedly essential to optimal physical performance.

Each vitamin performs a specific function in your body. The accompanying table lists the most important vitamins essential to successful motorsports performance.

Most types of athletes need extra vitamins for optimal performance. The physical demands of strength training and racing together use up these substances and make it more critical for replenishment. Caution must be taken, however, when fat-soluble vitamins (A, D, E, and K) are consumed in large quantities. These can be toxic.

Minerals

Until recently, vitamins were thought to be a more important concern in health and physical performance than minerals. Vast research now shows that minerals play a very significant role in various bodily functions essential to physical movement. A deficiency in any mineral can impair your physical and mental performance.

Let's take iron and potassium for example, because these minerals are commonly lacking in many diets. Failure to consume adequate amounts of these minerals can produce fatigue and weakness and possibly lead to injury.

Minerals are found in plants, animal foods, and your drinking water. All too often, the quantities of minerals found in these sources are too small. Since the stresses associated with motorsports and other strenuous physical activities promote the loss of various minerals, it becomes more important to increase your mineral intake. The best manner of mineral intake is through a good diet. Nutritional supplements are often warranted as well.

The accompanying table briefly describes some of the minerals important to physical performance.

Many factors affect the body's need for minerals. They include age, sex, genetics, medical history, occupation, and training. Often, the RDA simply does not take into account these factors affecting mineral demands.

Selected Vitamins, Their Function and Their Sources

This table clearly shows how a variety of foods should be included in your daily diet. Note that many vitamins are found in whole grains and vegetables.

Vitamin	Function	Source
Fat-Soluble		
A	Helps to maintain your skin and mucous membranes, and aids in night vision	Carrots and yellow leafy vegetables
D (Calciferol)	Regulates calcium and phosphate metabolism for stronger bones and teeth	Sunlight and milk
E (Tocopherol)	Numerous responsibilities, including red blood cell formation	Green leafy vegetables, whole grains, wheat germ, and vegetable oils
K (Menadione)	Blood clotting and bone metabolism	Green leafy vegetables, cheese, liver, and potatoes
Water-Soluble		
B_1 (Thiamin)	Carbohydrate metabolism and function of the nervous system	Whole grains, enriched bread and cereal, and poultry
B_2 (Riboflavin)	Aids in energy metabolism, and cell maintenance and repair	Milk, eggs, dark green vegetables, and whole-grain bread and cereal
B_3 (Niacin)	Various responsibilities; present in every cell in your body and helps in the reduction of high cholesterol	Poultry, whole grains, fish, meat, and green vegetables
B_5 (Pantothenic acid)	Aids in the formation of acetylcholine–the chemical involved in nerve transmission, memory, and the metabolism of energy	Poultry, fish, and whole grains
B_6 (Pyridoxine)	Involved in the metabolism of sugar, protein, and fat	Fish, wheat germ, poultry, and green leafy vegetables
B_{12} (Cobalamins)	Important in the metabolism of protein and fat, and helps in producing red blood cells	Liver, oysters, clams, milk, and meat
Folic acid (Folacin)	Aids in red blood cell formation	Green leafy vegetables, legumes, liver, and bran
Biotin	Helps to metabolize fats and carbohydrates	Brown rice, soybeans, green leafy vegetables, eggs, milk, and meat
C (Ascorbic acid)	Aids immune system function and combats free-radical activity	Citrus fruits and juices, and potatoes

Selected Minerals, Their Function, and Source

Mineral	Function	Source
Macro-Elements		
Calcium	Helps in the formation of teeth and bones and aids in nerve transmission, muscle contraction and relaxation, and contributes to heart action	Milk, cheese, green leafy vegetables, whole grains, and legumes
Magnesium	Essential to muscle contraction and relaxation, and aids in the transfer and release of energy	Whole grains, meat, milk, nuts, legumes, and raw green leafy vegetables
Phosphorus	Involved in bone formation, transport of fatty acids, energy production, and muscle contraction	Fish, poultry, whole grains, and legumes
Sodium	Helps in the transmission of nerve impulses and water balance within the body	Green leafy vegetables, table salt, milk, baking soda, and dried fruit
Potassium	Contributes to nerve transmission and muscle contraction	Whole grains, meats, fruits, vegetables, and legumes
Trace Elements		
Copper	Contributes to formation of bone, maintenance of the nervous system, and aids in converting iron to hemoglobin (oxygen-carrying agent in the blood)	Whole grains, meat, seafood, legumes, and foods cooked in copper skillets
Iron	Needed for sustaining and transporting oxygen in the blood	Meat, whole grains, enriched bread and cereal, dark green vegetables, legumes, and cooking in iron skillets
Manganese	Aids in protein metabolism, brain function, and glandular secretions	Green leafy vegetables, whole grains, tea, and legumes
Zinc	Responsible for cell growth, protein production, and aids in muscle contraction	Liver, seafood, eggs, milk, and whole grains

Water

Whether you know it or not, water is the most abundant substance in your body. Your muscles and brain are made up of more than 70 percent water, and the marrow of some bones (such as the sternum and ribs) contains as much as 75 percent of this substance. Water is considered by many to be the most important ingredient in your body. Without it, you cannot live long—say, maybe fourteen days. For race team members sweating profusely during a weekend's events, even greater amounts of water are needed on a daily basis to prevent dehydration. Intense exercise also contributes to an increased need for water.

Even a slight shortage of water can result in lessened performance and can lead to health problems. According to researcher C. Consolozio, you can lose as much as 10 percent of your strength with only a 3 percent loss of body fluids. Perhaps now you understand the importance of water in your daily diet.

3.10 How Much to Eat

It is likely that if you consume only good, low-fat foods containing complex carbohydrates and quality protein, you should never go hungry. Therefore, there is no need to gauge your food intake. This reasoning, however, does require an active lifestyle. Knowing how active those involved in racing generally are, and if a strength training regimen is undertaken, there's little if any doubt that you'll need to be concerned with how much you eat.

There *is,* however, an exception: if you make a practice of eating just before an inactive period, like before going to sleep. If you need to eat within two hours of retiring, you should consume a small meal consisting primarily of protein. Remember, a high-carbohydrate meal may prevent you from sleeping soundly.

But keeping in mind that the less active you are, the less you should eat, there is an alternative approach. By evaluating your activity level during the next three-hour period, you can gauge how much you should eat.

As world-renown fitness expert Fred Hatfield says: "Simply ask yourself: 'What am I going to do in the next three hours?'" By carefully evaluating your next three hours of activity, you can estimate approximately how much to eat at any particular meal. Obviously, the more active you are going to be, the more you should eat.

By consulting the table with the Glycemic Index Rating of Foods, you can select either the foods that will give you instant, but short-lived energy (a high glycemic index rating) or those that will give you prolonged energy (a low glycemic rating). You should attempt to select foods with a rating below 60 for the meals preceding your most active periods.

3.11 Are You Nutritionally Sound?

As a racer, you must realize the importance of all six major nutrients (carbohydrates, protein, fats, vitamins, minerals, and water). A deficiency or an excessive intake of these substances can be detrimental to your performance, and possibly your health. However, there are practical ways you can determine the status of your nutrition.

If your consumption of carbohydrates is too low, you will likely feel tired and weak and will easily fatigue when under physical stress. Since carbohydrates are the major source of energy, a low intake will render you with little available energy. You'll be lethargic and in severe cases, simply want to rest. Even your ability to reason and think will slowly diminish.

Although carbohydrates come in simple and complex flavors, a diet high in simple sugars is not much better for you than a diet without any carbohydrates at all. Sure, simple sugars (such as those found in candy bars) do provide instant energy, but it is short-lived. In fact, a candy bar can raise your blood-sugar quickly, but because candy is usually so highly concentrated in simple sugars, your body reacts by releasing insulin. When this happens, the insulin clears all the sugar from your blood and often leaves your blood-sugar levels lower than they were initially.

If you consume huge amounts of carbohydrates or you are not very active, the excess carbohydrates can be stored in your body as fat. Such is the case when a diet is high in simple rather than complex carbohydrates. But if you eat mostly complex carbohydrates, it is unlikely that fat storage will be promoted.

When you do not eat foods high in quality protein, again you can feel tired and weak. Remember, this nutrient is essential to the growth and development of various bodily tissues, especially your muscles, bones, and connective tissue. Your body is constantly in a state of rebuilding the cells of these tissues. A protein deficiency forces your body to work overtime rebuilding tissues and subsequently results in lowered resistance to infections and/or mental depression.

An overconsumption of protein can be disastrous to your waistline. It can stimulate a storage of excess protein calories as fat in your body. In addition, large amounts of protein consumed for prolonged periods can place a strain on your liver and kidneys, causing more frequent urination and possible organ damage.

Since most American diets already contain sufficient calories from fat, or rather *excessive* calories, a deficiency of fat intake is highly unlikely. In the event of a fat deficiency, your skin may become rough and your hair can lose some of its shine. Your blood pressure and cholesterol levels can rise. And since fat acts as a transport agent for the fat-soluble vitamins (A, D, E, and K), a very low fat intake can lead to a thinning and thus weakening of bones.

We all know the consequences of an excessive consumption of fat through your diet. It can lead to obesity and increased risk of arteriosclerosis, heart attack, and stroke. By carrying around excess poundage, you likely will have less enduring energy and strength and therefore reduced chances of success in any physical activity—including racing.

Vitamins and minerals do not give you energy, but they do contribute in many ways to the functions responsible for energy transfer and release in your body. They even contribute to muscular contraction. A deficiency in any of the major vitamins or minerals can lead to poor performance and health. But don't make the mistake others have. Make sure you are equally concerned about minerals as you are about vitamins. In fact, some experts believe that minerals may be the *more* important of the two. To perform your best in motorsports, you need to be concerned with all of these nutrients.

As illustrated in the accompanying vitamin source guide, an optimal intake of minerals is best approached through the consumption of various foods, most noticeably the whole grains, green leafy vegetables, and legumes.

One way you can be sure of getting adequate vitamins and minerals is to supplement your diet with them. This doesn't mean a handful of pills; it means a one-a-day multiple vitamin or mineral. Select one that meets nearly 100 percent of the RDA for most vitamins and minerals. For meeting your basic nutritional needs, you don't need the mega-packs containing a slew of pills that provide well over the RDA for many of these substances. But remember, this strictly means "for meeting your basic nutritional needs." Some vitamins and minerals may be needed in larger amounts. For instance, a high intake of the antioxidant vitamins C and E and beta-carotene may help to reduce damage done by free-radicals. (This was discussed at the beginning of this chapter.)

Review the tables in this chapter to see how a deficiency or overdose of selected vitamins and minerals affects your body's performance and functions.

Your need for water is unquestionable. Even a slight loss of body fluids can lead to significantly poorer performance. The most obvious problem with an inadequate water intake is dehydration, or lack of body fluids. This impairs numerous bodily functions, including a dangerous increase in deep-body temperature, an increase in blood viscosity (which leads to a subsequent risk for heart attack and stroke), and an additional strain on your liver to metabolize food. A lack of daily water intake can also reduce your strength and endurance.

It is interesting and surprising to note that you can get fat by not drinking enough water. Sounds ridiculous, but it isn't! Here's how it happens. The energy stored within your muscles and liver (glycogen) is stored with water. In fact, each gram of carbohydrate or glycogen is stored with three grams of water. Without the water, the glycogen circulates in your blood until your body decides to store it. If a deficiency of water is experienced, the glycogen is stored as are any other excess calories—as fat. As far as an overdose of water goes, don't worry, it cannot happen.

3.12 For Weight Loss

Don't concern yourself with the overall weight of your body—unless, of course, you compete in an event that requires you to be at a particular body weight. The major concern you should have is with the level of body fat you carry around day in and day out. To attempt weight loss, first you should throw away your bathroom scale. It is a misleading method of measurement for the health-conscious, exercising individual. Second, since we all like to see results from weight-loss programs, monitor your progress through a mirror, via a picture, or simply by the way your clothes fit. You may even wish to get some feedback from your "significant other," if you have one.

Because exercise, especially strength training, increases your fat-free weight (such as muscles and bones), it is possible for your body weight to remain the same or even increase when you're eating to lose weight (body fat). This is a result of increased weight of your muscles and bones, with a concomitant reduction in fat weight. (*Note:* Muscle tissue weighs more than fat tissue.) It is for this reason and this reason alone you were instructed to send your bathroom scale flying.

Fad diets and liquid diets—any type of diets—are unproductive and unsafe. Because most diets neglect some nutrients, you should not consider *any* of them for meal replacement. In fact, recent statistics show that nearly everyone on a commercial weight-loss diet regains most of the weight back within a year. Some even gain more back than they lost. However, there are a host of liquid meals capable of complementing smart eating when consumed as a snack. These drinks usually contain quality protein and complex carbohydrates with low amounts of fat.

As far as counting calories goes, it's simply not necessary. By reducing the fat in your diet, the total calories you consume is drastically lower. Fat has nearly twice the calories found in carbohydrates and protein. Each gram of fat contains nine calories, while carbohydrates and proteins each

Selected Vitamins: Signs of Deficiency and Overdose

The table lists selected vitamins and the possible consequences that could be experienced when these vitamins are lacking in your diet or consumed in excessive amounts.

Vitamin	Signs of Deficiency	Signs of Overdose
Fat-Soluble		
A	Rough skin, night blindness, and impaired resistance to infections	Headaches, fatigue, diarrhea, nausea, reduced appetite, and liver damage
D (Calciferol)	Bone weakness	Calcium deposits, nausea, increase in blood pressure and cholesterol, and reduced appetite
E (Tocopherol)	Rare	Possible nausea, fatigue, and headaches
K (Menadione)	Excessive bleeding and possible liver damage	Unknown in adults
Water-Soluble		
B_1 (Thiamin)	Muscle cramps, nausea. reduced appetite, and anxiety	May interfere with normal function of other B vitamins
B_2 (Riboflavin)	Fatigue, soreness of lips and mouth, and difficulty in swallowing	See vitamin B_1
B_3 (Niacin) sensation of skin	Skin rash	Increase in uric acid, high blood-sugar, nausea, and tingling
B_5 (Pantothenic acid	Unknown	See vitamin B_1
B_6 (Pyridoxine)	Convulsions, itchy skin	Possible dependency and depression
B_{12} (Cobalamins)	Anemia, weakness, and fatigue	See vitamin B_1
Folic acid (Folacin)	Impaired protein production and anemia	Unknown
Biotin	Rare; possible muscle pain, anemia, and insomnia	See vitamin B_1
C (Ascorbic acid)	Weakness, fatigue, anemia, and slowed healing	Urinary tract irritation, diarrhea, and kidney stones

Selected Minerals: Signs of Deficiency and Overdose

The chart shows selected minerals and subsequent conditions that could arise through a deficiency or overdose of any of these nutrients.

Mineral	Signs of Deficiency	Signs of Overdose
Macro-Elements		
Calcium	Weakening of bones	Drowsiness and calcium deposits
Magnesium	Muscle twitching and cramps, weakness, and irregular heart contractions	Possible impairment of nervous system if not in proper ratio to calcium
Phosphorus	Weakness, reduced appetite, and bone pain	Impaired calcium absorption
Sodium	Retention of water, muscle cramps, weakness, and headaches	Increase in blood pressure, kidney disease, and impaired heart action
Potassium	Muscle weakness, kidney failure, and irritability	Possible irregular heart action
Trace Elements		
Copper	Rare in adults	Vomiting and diarrhea
Iron	Anemia, weakness, fatigue, and headaches	Toxic buildup in liver
Manganese	Unknown	Unknown
Zinc	Impaired healing	Vomiting, nausea, and bleeding

contain four. So you can see how your total caloric intake is simply reduced through a reduction in dietary fat.

Believe it or not, it's not as difficult as you might think to lose weight. Just look at the sidebar in this chapter with the twelve health-conscious rules to follow for body-fat loss.

As we said earlier, keep in mind that you need to *eat* to lose weight. If you severely limit your food intake, you will be defeating the purpose of dieting. When an excessively low number of calories are consumed, your body protects itself from starvation by becoming more efficient. It virtually slows down your metabolism. By following the twelve dietary guidelines, you should never be hungry and you will lose those unwanted pounds.

The table gives some recommended examples of foods you can eat at respective meals and snacks.

3.13 For Weight Gain

The major difference between a diet designed for weight gain and a diet designed for weight loss is how much you eat. The extra calories must come from complex carbohydrates and quality protein, but still with a minimal amount of fat. Sure, you can easily increase your caloric intake by consuming more fat, but this would be unhealthy and unproductive to your performance.

When your interest is to gain weight, you should be concerned only with an increase in lean weight. Of most importance is the weight of your muscles and bones. The only way you can increase your body's demands for additional carbohydrates and protein is through resistance training, like that of strength training.

Again use a mirror, a picture, the way your clothes fit, or a significant other to determine your progress. A more scientific means would be through body-fat analysis. At present, skinfold calipers and underwater weighing techniques are most valid in determining your body fat and lean body weight.

Contrary to what many nutritionists believe, highly active individuals need additional sources of protein. An increasing number of scientific studies support this. Protein speeds up your recovery from strenuous physical work. And more often than not, protein intake does not meet the protein demands of exercise programs like strength training.

For the serious strength trainer who is giving 100 percent effort in training, the intake of dietary protein may need to be supplemented. Since dietary protein also contains some carbohydrates and fats, the only way you can restrict your consumption of unwanted food types is through supplementation. In the case of protein, protein powders and amino acid pills can provide you with quality protein without unwanted carbohydrates and fats. If you elect to consume supplementary protein, we recommend 100 percent egg protein sources. It is better used by your body than any other source of protein. But be cautious when consuming eggs for this purpose. The whites contain protein, while the yolks contain fat and cholesterol. You can simply discard the yolks when eating eggs.

At the same time, don't neglect the importance of carbohydrates. When you force your muscles to contract, time after time, under increasingly heavier workloads, your energy stores within your muscles and liver become depleted. The more intensely you train, the more they become depleted and thus the greater the demand for complex carbohydrates to refill these stores. We say *complex* carbohydrates not only because they sustain your energy levels, but also because they better refill your glycogen stores as compared to simple carbohydrates or sugars.

Weight-gain formulas can also aid in muscle growth and strength development. Most of these formulas contain high levels of protein along with carbohydrates. Many include unsaturated fats. Those formulas of interest to you should be the ones that provide large amounts of quality calories that can help to increase energy (through the carbohydrates) and rebuilding and growth (through the protein). But make sure you purchase those containing no fat or only small amounts of fat.

To gain weight while resistance training, whether it be strength training or bodybuilding, you must still adhere to healthy eating guidelines. Refer to the sidebar with the guidelines for gaining weight.

Don't lose perspective about what you are attempting to accomplish when trying to gain weight. What is important in racing is your strength-to-weight ratio. Your goal should be to get stronger and be healthy, but carry little body fat. And since stronger muscles are most often bigger muscles, your goals should be aimed at increasing muscle size. Don't be fooled into "bulking-up" by increasing the fat on your body. If you gain fat weight, your performance will suffer. In fact, so will your health.

Guidelines for Successful Weight Gain

Here are eleven healthful suggestions for gaining weight:

1. Eat five to six times a day, approximately every three hours. Consume your largest meal before the most active periods, and the smallest before sleep or inactivity. If you have time for only three meals a day, make sure your snacks are at least 200 calories. You might include weight-gain formulas for snacks, but try not to use them in place of meals.

2. Eat dried fruits for energy. They usually contain more calories than fresh fruit.

3. Consume large amounts of complex carbohydrates like pasta, potatoes, rice, beans, and whole-grain breads and cereals.

4. Snack on natural food bars rather than candy bars, but be sure to read the labels before purchasing these goods. Many "health foods" contain high amounts of fat.

5. Drink energy beverages containing mostly complex carbohydrates before and during your training and rigorous racing periods.

6. Consume breads containing fruit and grains such as banana bread, carrot cake, and oatmeal cookies.

7. Drink 100 percent fruit juice when you are thirsty.

8. Keep your dietary fat intake at a reasonable level. If you weigh less than 200lb, consume 10 to 15 grams of fat daily. If you weigh more than 200lb, consume 20-25 grams per day. Most of your fat intake should consist of unsaturated fats.

9. Consume at least 0.8 grams of protein per pound of body weight.

10. Eat the high-fat foods you crave no more than once every seven to ten days.

11. Exercise intensely to increase your body's demand for extra carbohydrates and protein.

3.14 Dealing with that Hypoglycemic Feeling

When you have not eaten for over three to four hours, your blood-sugar levels drop. A similar situation can be experienced following consumption of a candy bar or other foods containing high amounts of simple sugars. The end result is hypoglycemia or low blood-sugar, and subsequent feelings of weakness, nausea, irritability, and fatigue.

It makes sense that not eating lowers your blood-sugar. But exactly how does eating a candy bar produce the same reaction? Well, it goes like this: When foods having a high sugar content of simple carbohydrates are eaten, the sugar gets into your blood very quickly. This causes your body to overreact by producing more insulin than needed. Since insulin is responsible for the uptake of sugar into your cells, it virtually "wipes out" all the sugar in your blood. Then you are left with low or no blood-sugar. Just as if you had not eaten for hours.

If you attempt to drive a race vehicle, even if it's for just five seconds on a drag strip, chances are your performance will not be up to snuff if you're hypoglycemic. Reductions in performance will be increasingly noticeable during races taking more than five to ten minutes. The longer the race, the more you become affected. In fact, when you are physically active while being hypoglycemic, your thinking may become impaired and you may feel like you are going to pass out. Enough said on the potential problems arising from low blood-sugar and performance.

When you get these feelings associated with hypoglycemia, there are measures you can take to put sugar in your blood quickly. However, if you follow our smart eating recommendations, it is doubtful that you will ever experience hypoglycemia. But when your blood-sugar is low, you

Partial List of Recommended Foods for Healthy Eating

Breakfast
French toast (w/syrup only)
Whole-wheat pancakes
  (w/syrup only)
Toast with jam
Egg whites
Skim milk
100% fruit juice
Home fries (not fried in oil)
Coffee
Fruit plate
Whole-grain cereal

Lunch and Dinner
Chicken (white meat only)
Turkey (white meat only)
Beans
Baked potato
  (no butter or sour cream)
Rice
Peas
Apples, oranges
Yogurt (low-fat brands)
Lentils
Pasta (not egg noodles)
  (red sauce without meat)
Whole-wheat spaghetti
  (tomato sauce w/vegetables)

Snacks
Pretzels
Sponge cake
Fruit breads
Whole-grain cereals
Frozen yogurt (no-fat type)
Sherbet
Meal replacement drinks
  (low or no-fat brands)
Raw vegetables
Fruits
Popcorn (unbuttered)
Frozen 100%-fruit bars
Rice cakes

must immediately raise it through the consumption of sugars like fructose. Fructose is found in fruit and fruit juices. Although fructose is rated low on the Glycemic Index Rating scale, it enters your bloodstream very quickly. A meal high in complex carbohydrates should soon follow.

The most important consideration in dealing with hypoglycemia is to never provoke it to happen. And the most important consideration for any race driver, especially before a race, is to consume large amounts of low-glycemic foods. By looking at the table in this chapter, you can better determine what foods give you the most sustained energy.

3.15 Adjusting Your Nutrition During Injury

When you are injured, certain nutrients help you to heal. Carbohydrates can give you the energy needed to maintain general function of organs like your brain and heart. Fats help by transporting the fat-soluble vitamins A, D, E, and K. Protein aids in the repair of injured tissue. In addition, protein has an influence on your immune system, protecting against infection while increasing the speed of healing.

Without getting extremely complicated, we'll simply say that some of the amino acids cannot be used by your body without the help of certain vitamins and minerals. So, the best way to approach the matter is to guarantee optimal nutrition through proper eating.

When your bones are broken, your ligaments or tendons torn, or your muscles stretched out of shape, your body's demands for protein markedly increase. Remember, protein is responsible for rebuilding these tissues. And if quality protein, especially the essential amino acids, are lacking in your diet, it takes longer for your body to recover. In fact, we often have wondered why hospitals don't serve meals higher in protein than they normally do. It only makes sense. But perhaps they just don't realize the importance of protein in the diet.

Unfortunately, there's no "miracle" food that helps your recovery from injury. In basic terms, recovery from injury requires good nutrition—eating foods containing all of the six major nutrients: carbohydrates, protein, fats, vitamins, minerals, and water.

When your entire body is immobilized, it is vital that you reduce your total caloric intake. By reducing your activity level, your body's demand for calories declines. However, this is not to be confused with the increased need for nutrients during recovery. Rather, the need for quality nutrition is more significant. There's no room for "bad" nutrition. This means that your fat intake must still be low.

As you become more active, ideally you will need to increase the quantity (amount) of the high-nutrition foods you consume.

And when a single body part is immobilized, the quantity of nutritional foods consumed need not be reduced because you should remain active. Appropriate and perhaps modified activity virtually aids in the repair process. In fact, we recommend that you maintain your strength training program when a body part is unable to be used. Modifications will be needed, however. Chapter 5 goes into greater detail on the subject.

3.16 Nutrition for Recovery from Strenuous Exercise

Racers need to fully recover from the stresses associated with racing. Strength trainers need to fully recover from the stresses associated with intense, physical exercise. And when you do both, you must eat in a way that guarantees full recovery from both.

If you have been involved in motorsports for any length of time, it is likely that your nutritional habits have been dictated by your demanding work schedule. However, those who wish to get the most out of their strength training efforts should attempt to train intensely in order to enhance performance. When they do, a bigger rebuilding process must be facilitated and carbohydrates and protein are crucial agents in the process.

Improper nutritional practices can leave you weak, sore, and unproductive following workouts. The importance of smart eating is undeniable. The fact that hard-working athletes require additional nutritional support is equally undeniable.

The consumption of quality protein is an important requirement that's increasingly important for those who put forth a lot of effort during exercise. Research has shown that protein requirements increase as a result of demanding physical work.

While some individuals are attempting to gain lean body weight, others are trying to reduce their body weight. Both of these categories of individuals can benefit from quality dietary protein. For those interested in gaining fat-free weight, the hard work associated with heavy strength training places an even greater demand on diet for good, quality protein.

The best protein sources to include in your diet for recovery are egg whites, milk, and meat. The latter two should be of the low-fat variety. For instance: skim milk, and lean meat, chicken, and turkey (without skin).

Not only does your body require additional protein for the rebuilding of muscle tissue, but also your requirements for carbohydrates simultaneously increase. As your muscles work intensely, they burn glycogen stored inside the muscles and liver. The scientific world tells us that these energy stores must be refilled completely, in order to again perform maximal work. To do this, you need a diet that is high in complex carbohydrates. Since carbohydrates are responsible for refilling these energy stores, a higher intake of carbs might be necessary for future success in racing.

Recommended complex carbohydrates include whole-wheat spaghetti noodles with a meat-free tomato sauce, kidney beans, lentils, buckwheat pancakes, navy beans, sweet potatoes, apples, oranges, and skim milk.

Sports drinks that contain complex carbohydrates (usually maltodextrins) can also be used for speeding up recovery. The complex carbohydrates will stabilize in your blood, thus providing energy for the refilling of glycogen stores. Such drinks serve as a beneficial supplement to smart eating habits and help to ensure complete recovery following tough training sessions. If you consume these energy drinks during a race or during a workout, you should choose those containing a 7-10 percent concentration of carbohydrates. Lesser percentages will supply only small amounts of energy, while higher concentrations take longer to enter your bloodstream.

While undertaking a strenuous exercise program, your body's need for fats remains unchanged, but again, keep them to a minimum. Fat carries the fat-soluble vitamins A, D, E, and K throughout your body. These vitamins are essential to full recovery from exercise and other physically strenuous activities. In addition, a lack of fat-soluble vitamins to various cells of your body can lead to weakness and fatigue—something you should be feeling naturally after your vigorous workouts, but not from inadequate nutrition. So you do need some fat in your diet.

Your fat intake should consist of mostly unsaturated fats, from vegetable sources excluding palm, palm kernel, and coconut oils. Keep in mind that the process of hydrogenation makes unsaturated fats more saturated. It's the saturated fats that come from animal sources like meat and most dairy products that clog your arteries. Again, *read the labels.*

When you train, you can sweat away some valuable vitamins and minerals. When this happens day after day in absence of full replenishment, conditions like dehydration can develop. When that occurs, full recovery is impaired. Sports drinks containing the minerals often lost in sweating (electrolytes) can help by providing your body with fluids and nutrients. In addition, a multiple vitamin and mineral supplement is an effective way to replenish the vitamins and minerals lost through exercise.

But don't neglect your intake of water. In addition to helping refill carbohydrate stores within the muscles and liver, water helps to remove toxins and waste products resulting from intense training.

The accompanying table serves as a partial list of recommended foods that are low in fat and are healthy. Although the foods are categorized by traditional meals, there is no reason why breakfast foods cannot be eaten at lunch, and dinner foods substituted for breakfast.

3.17 Eating Before a Race

The last meal you eat before a race can either give you a boost or leave you lethargic and unprepared. If you are accustomed to eating a gourmet meal of, say, eggs and bacon or steak, with heavily buttered toast and whole milk before competing—you'd better think again. Although these foods *used* to be the choices of athletes before a big contest, they are now considered, or rather proven, to be taboo.

Even though every meal should be low in fat, without question your pre-race meal should be very low in fat. Because those foods listed as the traditional athletic pre-game meal are high in fat, they take longer to digest and to be absorbed by the body tissues (assimilation). As a result, blood flow is directed away from the muscles and brain to favor the digestion process in the gastrointestinal tract. This shift in blood flow can cause cramps, vomiting, and fatigue when physical activity is performed soon after eating such foods.

There are nine basic rules to follow when eating your pre-race meal. This applies not only to drivers, but also to the pit crew and others who perform duties during a race.

1. Consume your last meal two or three hours before preparing for a race. This permits complete digestion and assimilation.

2. Don't eat foods high in fat. Remember, they take longer to digest and are not healthy choices. This includes foods prepared in grease, butter, margarine, and other oils and fats.

3. Stay away from spicy foods. They can upset your stomach, causing nausea and possible cramps and diarrhea.

4. Do not consume foods high in protein for at least eight hours prior to a race. The waste products resulting from protein digestion will not likely need to be excreted during strenuous physical activity.

5. Eat foods that are rated low on the Glycemic Index Rating scale. (Refer to the table for suggestions.) These are complex carbohydrates such as whole grains, some vegetables, fruits, pancakes, and waffles. But forget the butter and margarine often placed on some of these foods. Small amounts of syrup are OK, though. When selecting carbohydrates for this meal, choose those that don't contain large amounts of fiber. Since fiber speeds the elimination process, which surely

would be an unfavorable situation, you might select foods made of processed grains like pasta for the majority of your meal.

6. Restrict your consumption of simple carbohydrates (sugars). A large intake of simple sugars produces hypoglycemia or low blood-sugar. Examples include table sugar, candy, honey, cake, and cookies.

7. Be consistent with the foods you eat. It is not wise to experiment with unfamiliar foods before a race. They may be detrimental to your performance.

8. Don't skip meals. You need to completely refill all energy stores of your body. This cannot possibly be done in a single meal.

9. Limit your salt intake by avoiding the likes of table salt, soy sauce, canned soups, relish, catsup, smoked meats and fish, as well as other more obviously salted foods like potato chips.

3.18 Eating on the Run

A racer's life is nonstop. You're always on the go. Whether you're a part-time racing enthusiast or a full-time mechanic, your time is valuable. And who always has the time to stop, prepare a meal, and sit down to quietly eat it? Our guess is no one.

Principles of smart eating always need to be followed, even if you don't have time to prepare a seven-course meal. Your body doesn't know when you don't have time to eat and it really doesn't care, for that matter. Your body's nutritional needs remain high, especially if you are active, and more so if you strength train.

With all of this in perspective, you can now see why you should never skip meals. Research shows that your metabolism can slow down if you don't eat regularly. In fact, the most often skipped meal is also the worst to skip—breakfast. Skipping breakfast alone can contribute to slowing your metabolism. In addition, breakfast eaters generally burn more calories during the entire day and tend to be more inclined to consume less fat during the day. Just think about it: Literally, breakfast means "breaking a fast." The fast is facilitated through not eating for hours during sleep, rendering you low blood-sugar upon awakening. By eating when you arise, you are virtually breaking this fast by putting essential energy into your bloodstream.

It is also a fact that those who skip meals often accomplish less work, are slower to make decisions, and fatigue more quickly. There is another reason why it is so important to eat approximately every three hours. When you eat less often, your blood-sugar levels drop. Not only does this produce hypoglycemia, it also affects your brain. Glucose, the sugar that floats around in your blood, provides the energy or fuel from which your brain operates. This is precisely why you should not skip breakfast.

How can you make time to eat without wasting valuable time cooking? And who said you had to sit down to a formal meal setting in order to eat, anyway? The answer to both of these questions is, *you don't have to!* You can eat on the run.

The time you spend getting ready for work in the morning can also be spent eating—a mouthful here and a mouthful there. Your body doesn't mind. Since most of us drive or take a bus to work, why not utilize that time to eat? Even the time it takes you to walk to your car can be spent eating and walking. Time spent working at your desk or running between meetings is ample time to down a healthy sandwich. If you want something badly enough, you'll find the time to get it.

However, taking a break when it's time to eat can act as a stress release and help to clear your mind. Undoubtedly, it is more enjoyable and may contribute to your being more conscious about what you are eating.

By preparing foods (when time allows) ahead of time, you can simply zap them in a microwave or leave them in the refrigerator, ready to grab and eat. Prepared meals packaged in a microwaveable container can easily and quickly be reheated in a microwave oven. Refrigerated sandwiches are especially handy and serve as good alternatives to not eating or having to spend time cooking. Whenever you have one hand free, you can easily feed yourself while doing almost anything. You can make your sandwiches more healthy by adding vegetables to a protein-rich food (like chicken or turkey) and placing everything on whole-grain bread for enhanced energy. Forget the fat-filled condiments.

You can stash healthy snacks in your briefcase or you can brown-bag it. A handheld cooler is also beneficial. Just make sure your food choices are healthy. That is, your food provides all six essential nutrients needed by your body: carbohydrates, protein, fat (in low amounts), vitamins, minerals, and water.

The accompanying table contains some healthy suggestions for eating five times a day when you don't have much time. By no means does the "at least" column satisfy all your nutrition needs.

Looking at these suggestions, you can see how easy it is to eat healthy when you are on the run. With the possible exceptions of the "A Better Choice" entries for breakfast and dinner, you can eat while performing other duties. But even these two exceptions can be precooked at an earlier time, then reheated and eaten in less than ten minutes.

Planning is a major concern when dealing with eating on the run. If you prepare foods ahead of time, they can quickly be ready to eat. But when you don't plan for what you are going to eat, you're likely to skip meals. This can result in the subsequent robbing of any local vending machines of unhealthy, fat-filled foods. You should plan ahead by making a grocery list before shopping at the market. Believe us, you will be more inclined to purchase healthy foods rather than those that stimulate your often overpowering sweet tooth.

3.19 Eating on the Road

Most times it is just not practical to carry additional baggage for food while traveling. However, you can easily transport premixed sports beverages containing complex carbohydrates and quality protein. But this should not constitute your entire diet while away from home.

What *can* be done is to learn how to eat healthy at fast-food chains and other family-type restaurants. Almost all restaurants serve some healthy foods. It may be up to you. You may need to place your order with certain specifications. It's like the engine in your vehicle. You follow specific guidelines to comply with the rules of the sport and still manipulate the engine's performance.

The accompanying table contains just a few suggestions for foods made healthy through specialized ordering. Although you can eat anything at any time, we will gear these suggestions to the three traditional meal schedules (breakfast, lunch, and dinner). You should already know what foods can be eaten for healthy snacks between meals.

As you can see, by dictating your specifications to most food orders, you can make them healthier. There are other specifications you can follow, too. For instance, you can make any sandwich healthier by having the cook or chef use rye or pumpernickel bread or whole-wheat rolls, whole-grain pita pockets, or rice cakes, rather than white bread.

You can add various vegetables and fruit to nearly any prepared food to make it more nutritious. Lettuce, spinach leaves, tomatoes, carrots, and sliced apples can make any sandwich or plate of food taste better. Even cooking with onions and peppers can make most meats and potatoes a gourmet meal.

The major problem that occurs with making healthy food unhealthy is when fat-laden condiments are added. For instance, a baked potato is healthy, but when it is drowned with butter and sour cream, the fat content soars. You can make a baked potato taste like it is complemented with these fatty condiments by replacing them with the likes of no-fat imitation butter (one brand is Butter Buds) and no-fat plain yogurt. It may not sound tasty, but it sure does the trick.

Soups are another misleading food. Many of those that are oh so tasty are made with cream. Consume these in moderation—they contain loads of fat. You can even be somewhat healthy when selecting desserts. Obviously most of them contain high levels of fat, so be careful. Fruit is a fine alternative to most high-fat desserts. Fruits can be complemented with no-fat yogurt (frozen or regular) and can satisfy your sweet-tooth cravings.

When it comes to beverages, be selective. If a restaurant serves milk, make sure it is skim milk or, at most, 1 percent. And don't be misled with the term "juice." Make sure it is 100 percent fruit juice. Those labeled "drinks" or "punches" usually contain very little real juice, but have loads of simple sugars in them.

In the world of racing, many of those involved don't always have the time to sit down to eat a complete meal in a restaurant. But everyone has time to visit a fast-food restaurant. These are the restaurants that traditionally have been known to serve high-fat foods, although they are becoming more and more health conscious.

We have established a chart that you may be interested in posting in your racing garage or on your toolbox for future reference. The chart illustrates some of the country's major fast-food chain menus. By no means does this chart include every item found on each fast-food restaurant's menu. We have rated selected foods by the amount of fat found in them.

Our rating system labels the selected foods by way of four basic recommendations for consumption. These are:

ANY—anytime (less than 5 grams of fat) for consumption almost anytime

OCC—occasional consumption (8-9 grams)

SEL—seldom to be eaten (13-14 grams), and

HEV—hardly ever eaten (more than 44 grams)

In addition, those foods containing more than 1,000 but less than 2,000 milligrams (mg) of sodium have been so indicated with an asterisk following respective ratings. Those foods containing 2,000mg or more of sodium are indicated with two asterisks.

The table lists foods with recommended consumption frequencies. The rating ANY (anytime) means just that—not *all the time*. The OCC (occasional) rating is reflective of up to twice a week consumption. The rating of SEL (seldom) means once a week consumption at most. And HEV (hardly ever) reflects recommendations of consumption no more than once every ten to fourteen days.

There it is. All you need to know to eat properly—in black and white. There's no excuse for not being smart about the way you eat. Our smart eating plan may seem difficult at first, but it's our guess that within two weeks, you'll have no problems with it. This chapter serves as an educational tool. After reading it, you should be able to determine which foods are good for you and which are not, and how often you can eat your favorite "bad" foods.

Healthy Suggestions for Eating Five Times a Day

	At Least...	**A Better Choice**
Breakfast:	Low-fat muffin Skim milk	Hard-boiled egg whites Whole-wheat bread and jam Whole-grain cereal w/skim milk Fruit Coffee
Snack:	Apple	Apple Skim milk
Lunch:	Chicken or turkey sandwich (on whole-wheat bread w/mustard and lettuce) Skim milk	Chicken or turkey sandwich (on whole-wheat bread w/ mustard and alfalfa sprouts) 100% fruit juice Skim milk
Snack:	100% fruit juice	Celery sticks 100% fruit juice Whole-grain bagel
Dinner:	Chef salad 100% fruit juice Skim milk	Broiled fish Baked potato Vegetable salad 100% fruit juice Skim milk

Specialized Ordering Recommendations

	As Seen on Menu...	**Your Specifications**
Breakfast:	Eggs and bacon, ham or sausage w/toast and coffee Milk	Egg whites with no butter Lean piece of ham Whole-wheat toast w/out butter Coffee black or w/1% or skim milk Skim milk or 100% fruit juice
Lunch:	Chicken sandwich on white bread w/mayonnaise Salad with dressing Orange juice, fruit punch, or grape drink	Chicken (white meat) on whole-wheat with mustard Vegetable salad with no-fat or low-fat dressing or vinegar only 100% orange juice
Dinner:	Chef salad Pasta w/tomato sauce or meat sauce	Chef salad with only turkey, chicken, and a few slices of cheese Pasta w/tomato sauce

Fast-Food Restaurant Scoreboard

(a partial list of fast-foods)

Item(s) and Associated Restaurant	Rating
Complete Meals	
Breakfast:	
Cheerios, milk, orange juice, bran muffin (McDonald's)	ANY
Bran muffin, orange juice (Carl's Jr.)	OCC
Pancakes w/syrup and margarine, juice, milk (Hardee's)	SEL*
Sunrise Sandwich w/sausage, hash browns, milk (Carl's Jr.)	HEV*
Big Country Breakfast w/sausage, juice, milk (Hardee's)	HEV**
Lunch/Dinner:	
Baked fish, light, two pieces, rice, salad (no dressing) (Long John Silver's)	ANY
BK Broiler, side salad (no dressing), juice (Burger King)	OCC
Quarter Pounder w/Cheese, large fries, chocolate shake, apple pie (McDonald's)	HEV*
Famous Star Burger, zucchini, cookie, soda (Carl's Jr.)	HEV**
Extra Tasty Crispy three-piece dinner (Kentucky Fried Chicken)	HEV**
Double Big Classic w/Cheese, large Frosty, Biggie fries, chocolate chip cookie (Wendy's)	HEV**
Separate Menu Items	
Breakfast:	
Orange or grapefruit Juice, six-ounce	ANY
Cheerios, 3/4 cup	ANY
Apple bran muffin, fat-free (McDonald's)	ANY
Onion bagel (Dunkin' Donuts)	ANY
English muffin with margarine (Carl's Jr.)	ANY
Donut, jelly filled (Dunkin' Donuts)	OCC
Croissant, plain (Burger King)	OCC
Hotcakes w/margarine and syrup (McDonald's)	OCC
Biscuit (Arby's)	SEL
Egg McMuffin (McDonald's)	SEL
Danish, average (Burger King)	SEL
Big Breakfast (eggs, sausage, biscuit, w/spread, hash browns) (McDonald's)	HEV*

Item(s) and Associated Restaurant	Rating
Hamburgers:	
Jr. Hamburger (Wendy's)	OCC
Hamburger (McDonald's)	OCC
McLean Deluxe (McDonald's)	OCC
Hamburger (Burger King)	SEL
Happy Star Hamburger (Carl's Jr.)	SEL
Cheeseburger (McDonald's)	SEL
Hamburger, single (Dairy Queen)	SEL
Cheeseburger (Hardee's)	SEL
Real Lean Deluxe (Hardee's)	SEL
Hamburger (Wendy's)	SEL
McLean Deluxe with Cheese (McDonald's)	SEL
Double Whopper with Cheese (Burger King)	HEV*
Double Western Bacon Cheeseburger (Carl's Jr.)	HEV*
Roast Beef Sandwiches:	
BBQ Roast Beef Sandwich (Dairy Queen)	ANY
Roast Beef, junior (Arby's)	OCC
French Dip roast beef sandwich (Arby's)	SEL
Roast Beef, regular (Hardee's)	SEL
Roast Beef, regular (Arby's)	SEL
Big Roast Beef (Hardee's)	SEL*
Ham/Steak Sandwiches:	
Ham Sandwich, six-inch (Subway)	SEL
Steak Sandwich, six-inch (Subway)	SEL
Hot Ham 'N' Cheese Sandwich (Hardee's)	SEL*
Country Fried Steak Sandwich (Carl's Jr.)	HEV*
Fish:	
Shrimp, Homestyle, one-piece (Long John Silver's)	ANY
Shrimp, battered, one-piece (Long John Silver's)	ANY
Fish, Homestyle, one-piece (Long John Silver's)	OCC
Tuna sandwich, six-inch (Subway)	SEL
Clams, breaded (Long John Silver's)	SEL
Seafood and crab sandwich, six-inch (Subway)	SEL*
Fish, battered, one-piece (Long John Silver's)	SEL
Chicken and Turkey:	
Charbroiler BBQ Chicken Sandwich (Carl's Jr.)	ANY
Chicken Fajita (McDonald's)	OCC

continued on next page

Item(s) and Associated Restaurant	Rating
Original Recipe Drumstick (Kentucky Fried Chicken)	OCC
Chicken Littles Sandwich (Kentucky Fried Chicken)	OCC
Chicken Stix, six-pieces (Hardee's)	OCC
BK Broiler Chicken Sandwich (Burger King)	OCC
Grilled Chicken Sandwich (Hardee's)	OCC
Grilled Chicken Sandwich (Wendy's)	OCC
Turkey sandwich, six-inch (Subway)	OCC
Chicken Tenders, six pieces (Burger King)	SEL
Chicken McNuggets, six pieces (McDonald's)	SEL
Original Recipe Center Breast (Kentucky Fried Chicken)	SEL
Potatoes (baked and other preparations):	
Baked potato, plain	ANY
Mashed potatoes and gravy (Kentucky Fried Chicken)	ANY
Cheese potato (Wendy's)	SEL
Bacon and cheese potato (Carl's Jr.)	HEV*
Potatoes (fried):	
Fries, one order (Long John Silver's)	ANY
Hash brown potatoes (McDonald's)	OCC
French fries, small (McDonald's)	SEL
French fries, regular (Kentucky Fried Chicken)	SEL
Potato Cakes (Arby's)	SEL
Tater Tenders (Burger King)	SEL
French fries, small (Wendy's)	SEL
Hash Rounds (Hardee's)	SEL

Label	Fat Content	Consumption Recommendatons
ANY	less than 5 grams of fat	Almost Anytime
OCC	8-9 grams of fat	Occasionally
SEL	13-14 grams of fat	Seldom
HEV	more than 44 grams of fat	Hardly Ever
*	contains 1,000-1,999 mg of sodium	
**	contains 2,000 mg or more of sodium	

Item(s) and Associated Restaurant	Rating
Desserts:	
Frozen yogurt cone, low-fat (McDonald's)	ANY
Yogurt cone, large (Dairy Queen)	ANY
Frozen yogurt sundae, strawberry, low-fat (McDonald's)	ANY
DQ Sandwich (Dairy Queen)	ANY
Cool Twist cone, chocolate (Hardee's)	ANY
Sundae, chocolate, regular (Dairy Queen)	OCC
Apple turnover (Hardee's)	SEL
Banana split (Dairy Queen)	SEL
Big Cookie (Hardee's)	SEL
Cool Twist sundae, hot fudge (Hardee's)	SEL
Apple pie (Burger King)	SEL
Shakes:	
Milk, skim	ANY
Milk, 1% low-fat	ANY
Milk, 2% low-fat	ANY
Shake, low-fat, average (McDonald's)	ANY
Shake, average (Hardee's)	OCC
Shake, vanilla (Arby's)	SEL
Shake, chocolate, regular (Burger King)	SEL
Salads and Dressings:	
Side Salad (Burger King)	ANY
Three Bean Salad, 1/4-cup	ANY
Garden Salad (Wendy's)	ANY
Salad Dressing, Lite Vinegarette (McDonald's)	ANY
Chunky Chicken Salad (McDonald's)	ANY
Coleslaw (Kentucky Fried Chicken)	ANY
Ocean Chef Salad (Long John Silver's)	ANY
Turkey Salad, small (Subway)	OCC
Chef Salad (McDonald's)	OCC
Chef Salad (Burger King)	OCC
Chicken Fiesta Salad (Hardee's)	SEL

Key: This system rates foods according to fat content and our subsequent recommendations regarding frequency of consumption. In addition, an asterisk (*) next to the rating indicates 1,000-1,999 milligrams of sodium found in the food product. Two asterisks (**) indicate more than 2,000 milligrams of sodium present.

Chapter 4

The Pit Crew and the Iron Game

Regularity is the key to exercise. You cannot be successful at anything unless your efforts are consistent. Self-control and dedication are the factors that form consistency, and consistency is a quality all champions display.

Regularity is the key to exercise. You cannot be successful at anything unless your efforts are consistent. Self-control and dedication are the factors that form consistency. It's a quality all champions display.

4.1 Reducing Injuries in the Pits and Garage

Not all types of pit crew and mechanical duties include speedy performance on pit lane. Some quick performance is needed between heats of short-term, intense racing like that seen in sprint car, monster truck, and speedboat racing. However, more of the time is spent in the garage—either at the racetrack or back at the office.

Regardless of whether time is of the essence while the race vehicle is being worked on, strenuous work is common for mechanics and crew members. Mechanics constantly bend over the race machine, making adjustments, replacing parts, building and rebuilding. They lift and twist, lie on their backs, kneel, stand, and sometimes sit. Almost every movement they perform requires some type of strength. Without it, even the slightest injury becomes more possible.

The major difference that pit crew members and mechanics experience during pit stops of a race versus the work done in the garage is speed of movement. It's quite obvious, fast movements place you at greater risk of getting injured. Because movements that are performed at high speed place more stress on the muscles, tendons, ligaments, and bones, strength training should be a prerequisite for all pit crew members for preventing injury and improving performance. You

might escape injury in pit lane simply by having more speed to get out of dangerous situations.

Take, for example, running to and from a race car during a NASCAR Winston Cup race. If you are not fast on your feet, pit times can easily surpass 20 seconds (sec). Trying to be fast without proper physical conditioning can result in the likes of a sprained ankle, torn cartilage in the knee, or even a strained back. In addition, in NASCAR or Indy racing, where quick pit stops are of the utmost importance, 20-plus second pit stops can cost a car plenty of valuable places—you can go from first to twentieth in a matter of 5sec.

Not only is running speed important to pit stop times, but the performance of your actual duties (changing a tire, for instance) needs to be done in a timely fashion, too. Just imagine if you were responsible for changing a tire during a pit stop and did so at the same speed as your local tire dealer. You'd be out of a job. Or take a hydroplane speedboat pit crew member who is required to help change gears and engines during a 1 hour (hr) period between heats. Speed of all physical movements is necessary, and it's the functional strength obtained through effective strength training that enables you to move with speed.

But let's not be solely concerned with pit stops. The work you do in the garage also requires a good amount of strength. If your back is weak, as so many are, constant bending, lifting, and twisting can lead to strains and sprains and thus poor performance and that old annoying sensation—pain. This is all too common.

Although injury can occur when you overexert yourself (as can occur from lifting heavier objects

This picture shows the performance intensity that's required on pit lane during a green light pit stop in a NASCAR Winston Cup race. This picture was taken during a pit crew competition, but virtually the same procedures take place during races. Although some forms of *racing do not have pit stops, many do incorporate several heats, motos, or other qualifiers when engine changes, gear changes, and other repairs must be handled quickly. It's easy to see how proper exercise can aid in the speedy performance of all crew members.*

than you should), it sometimes is the smaller, lighter, and repetitive duties that lead to injury.

When you perform any type of work, your muscles virtually break down. If repetitive movements are performed every day, and complete recovery is not facilitated through proper diet and rest, chances are you are going to be injured. It doesn't necessarily take heavy, intense work to cause injuries.

As microtrauma (small degrees of damage to the muscles) occurs during both repetitive and intense heavy physical work, tissues become weaker and thus more vulnerable to becoming torn or strained. When full recovery is not permitted, injury in the form of tendinitis and strains is often experienced.

To develop strong tissues is the best means of preventing such injury resulting from either overexertion or overuse. If you possess ample strength in the complete range of motion, your chances of becoming injured while performing

such motorsports duties will undoubtedly be reduced.

Your body is similar to the machine you work on. If you use quality parts in your vehicle, you are less likely to experience breakdown and accidents. So it is with your body: if you use quality parts (if you develop strong body parts), chances are you won't break down and become injured.

The information provided in chapters 1 and 2 applies not only to drivers, but also to anyone involved in physical work—on and in a race vehicle as well as in anything you do. It's best to think of strength training as a benefit to performance, and also as a means of preventing bodily breakdown or injury.

4.2 Improving Agility

Agility can be defined as the ability to perform several quick movements in opposing directions—like running around a race vehicle or placing a jack under the vehicle during a pit stop. You need a good foundation of strength in order to be agile in your physical movements.

To improve your agility even more, you need power. Remember, power is the ability to exhibit strength in a fast manner. Power is responsible for foot and leg action during quick starts and stops as well as changes in direction. From a physiological perspective, such movement is a product of nerve and muscle function. Because nerve-muscle interaction can be enhanced through proper physical activity, that is, strength and power-speed training, anyone wishing to improve their performance in the pits and in the garage should partake in the iron game.

Strength training alone helps to improve the control of bodily movements. Since every movement you perform requires a message to be sent to your muscles, from your brain via your nerves, any functional improvement of these tissues will improve your ability to move. Proper physical training contributes to such improvement in tissue functioning. But even though proper training helps, you still have a need for skill. By combining strength training (and power-speed training) with skill training (actual performance of duties), chances of reaching your goals will increase. Do you realize how much skill (and strength) is involved in mounting a 600lb-plus tire onto a monster truck?

But it's the fast, powerful raising of a resistance during power-speed training that "teaches" your muscles to respond the fastest. For someone who needs to reach a certain destination in a short time (such as pit crew members running to a race car during a pit stop), this means properly performed squats or leg presses, stiff-leg dead lifts (with an arched back), and calf raises. Keep in mind: The manner in which you exercise your muscles determines how the respective muscles will respond during your performance.

As you probably already know, if you're not prepared to do even a slightly strenuous job, you can easily get hurt. You can have all the strength you need, but if you are not coordinated in the movements necessary for job functioning, injury is more likely.

Chapter 8 gives some examples of workouts designed specifically for the pit crew.

Chapter 5

Getting 100 Percent Out of Your Strength Training

In all the world of motorsports, the most important consideration is performance—both physical and mental. By doing the right things— getting in peak condition, following smart eating habits, controlling stress, allowing for adequate rest and choosing the best types of training techniques— your chances of success are greatly enhanced.

In the world of motorsports, the most important consideration is performance, both physical and mental. By doing the right things—getting in peak condition, following smart eating habits, controlling stress, allowing for adequate rest, and choosing the best types of training techniques—your chances of success are greatly enhanced.

5.1 Your Strength Training Program

When you begin a strength training program, you shouldn't dive into it haphazardly, with no direction and only a purpose. It has to be systematic, just like your driving. In racing, if you didn't have a system of procedures to follow, your efforts would have little reward. In essence, you'd flop!

You should always begin any type of exercise program with a doctor's approval. This helps to rule out any underlying causes for injury or illness.

We classify nine muscle groups as major movers. That is, they are responsible for most movements involved in daily living. When we refer to a strength training program for performance drivers, we are concerned with a minimum of twelve muscle groups. These are the muscles most involved in driving any race vehicle. But when we talk about an optimal strength training program for race drivers, we are concerned with fourteen major muscle group exercises. These are the exercises most affecting the muscle groups used in almost every movement any type of racer will likely need to perform, whether it be in motocross, NASCAR, or monster truck racing.

The muscles used in racing are those that should receive major emphasis in all racers' strength training programs, and a minimum of one exercise per muscle group is essential to generate distinct benefits. The accompanying table illustrates the major muscle groups that should be included in a general conditioning program and a program designed specifically for drivers. The racing program is listed in two categories: a minimum and an optimal program. You might want to check out the muscle chart in this book to locate muscles referred to in the table. The table's right column serves only as a sample of the specific movements produced by the respective muscles during performance driving. Keep in mind, these are only examples. Each muscle is used in numerous other racing duties.

As you can see by studying the accompanying table, the driver must strengthen and tone more muscles than someone simply involved in general conditioning. Not only does the strengthening of these muscles reflect improved performance, it is also essential in preventing injury. For instance, by exercising the trapezius and spinal erector muscles, your spinal column is better protected from injury. Since the spinal column houses the spinal cord, this is a vital protective measure to prevent serious injury, perhaps so serious that it could result in paralysis.

Obviously, this optimal program gives the most benefits for a performance driver, but it also takes slightly more time to perform. But it's like anything else you do: The more you put into it, the more you get out of it—as long as you do it correctly.

Major Muscles or Muscle Groups for Involvement in Strength Training

Primary Muscle or Muscle Group Affected	General Conditioning Program	Motorsports Driver Minimum	Optimal	Selected Applications in Driving
Quadriceps	*	*	*	Support body during motocross racing
Hamstrings	*	*	*	Help to lift foot off clutch
Pectorals	*	*	*	Aid in moving hand across body to turn steering wheel
Anterior deltoid			*	Contributes to the support of hands on steering wheel
Lateral deltoid (aka medial deltoid)	*	*	*	Helps maintain arm position on steering wheel or handlebars
Posterior deltoid			*	Aids in coordinated movement of turning steering wheel or handlebars
Trapezius		*	*	Helps to support head and neck
Latissimus dorsi	*	*	*	Assists arm movement while shifting
Spinal erectors (most notable: iliocostalis lomborum muscle)		*		Protect lower back
Biceps	*	*	*	Help cushion forces of upper body movement when returning to the ground after jumping a mogul in motocross
Triceps	*	*	*	Same as biceps above
Gastrocnemius	*	*	*	Permits foot to push down on brake, accelerator, and clutch
Wrist flexors		*	*	Help to control steering wheel, handlebars, and shifter
Abdominals	*	*	*	Contribute to support of spine
Total number of muscle groups	9	12	14	

In addition, racers must have strong wrists. If you've ever raced, you know how much work it takes to maintain control of the steering wheel or handlebars when traveling at high speeds or while hitting the ground after being airborne.

There are three major factors affecting the number of exercises you should perform during strength training. First, your goals. If you truly want your strength training to have a significant impact on your racing performance, you will be required to strengthen all of the major muscle groups involved. This takes some time.

The second factor is time availability. In order to perform all recommended strength training exercises, you will need to dedicate between 45 and 60 minutes (min) for each exercise session. Strength training should be "short 'n sweet." It's quality, not necessarily quantity, that's a primary concern. If time is severely limited, fewer exercises may be required and subsequent results likely reduced. It then becomes more important than ever to include appropriate exercises in your program.

The third factor involves exercise tolerance; not everyone *likes* to exercise. Some don't mind, but like to get it over with quickly. How well you tolerate exercise also helps to determine how many exercises you must perform. This is especially important when selecting exercises that help you accomplish your specific goals.

It is also essential that you perform exercises to increase your strength in the extreme ranges of motion. When exercises like the bench press are performed for strengthening chest muscles, you must also include an exercise like the flye to stress these muscles in their completely stretched position. By performing the bench press only, you will lose flexibility in your chest and shoulder area and risk injury to these muscles as well as your shoulder joint. This will, therefore, increase the number of exercises you will need to do.

The accompanying table gives examples of some strength training exercises and the body parts that each exercise affects the most.

The table constitutes only a partial list of possible exercises you can perform for each of the muscle groups needed to be strengthened for improving your driving performance and reducing risks of injury. The exercises are listed in order of muscle size and for the most part, in the order in which they should be performed.

5.2 Hows and Whys of Warm-ups

It's common to see a weekend jogger on the side of the road stretching in a hurdler's position. It is also common to see professional football players touching their toes before a game. But how often do you see a NASCAR driver or any other race enthusiast warming up before a race? What most people do not realize is that warm-ups can improve performance. And there is a big difference in how you warm up for various activities.

Stretching and warming up do improve physical performance, along with reducing risk of injury. Racers and pit crew members are no exception to this rule, whether the warm-ups are done before a race or before a workout. However, stretching will be more practical for a driver before a race.

In fact, many strength training athletes can tell you of at least one time in their career, perhaps when time was short, that injury prevailed as a result of neglected warm-ups. No doubt you have often seen athletes as well as general fitness buffs vigorously performing jumping jacks prior to beginning their workouts. But does it really help?

Warm-ups are often classified by their ability to increase temperature within the body. The rise in temperature is a result of increased blood flow along with various metabolic functions. Warm-ups are categorized into three types: passive, general, and specific.

Passive-type warm-ups increase your body (core) temperature through some outside means, like a sauna or steam room.

With general-type warm-ups, your body's core temperature rises due to a general, nonspecific series of movements like jumping jacks. During jumping jacks, for instance, the shoulder, hip, and ankle joints increase in blood flow and thus temperature. This movement does little or nothing to increase blood supply to the muscles, of say, your back.

The third category, specific-type warm-ups, increase your core temperature and the blood flow (and thus temperature) to the working muscles. During strength training exercise this means a "warm-up set" of the same exercise to be performed, done with the use of light resistance (weight) and a moderate to high number of repetitions (for example, ten to twenty reps). This prepares specific muscles and tendons for the work ahead by increasing blood flow to these tissues along with stimulating them to possess greater elasticity. The result is a significantly reduced risk of injury to the tissues.

Depending on your activity level, all forms of warm-ups might be important. To anyone involved in strength training or selected activities in racing, specific-type warm-ups take precedence.

There are many physiological responses to warm-ups. For example, because of the increase in intramuscular temperature, oxygen is more rapidly released from its storage with myoglobin (within the muscles) and hemoglobin (within the blood). As the viscosity of a muscle lessens (thought we were talking about oil, didn't you?), there is a concomitant increase in speed and force of a single muscle contraction. In fact, this might be better explained through the analogous relationship of motor oil to a car. The more the oil heats up, the less viscous it gets and the better it penetrates throughout the running motor. It's the same way with your muscles. As you warm up, the resulting increases in temperature produce more efficient movement.

On the cellular level, a rise in muscle temperature produces accelerated metabolic reactions. This means that local metabolite (waste products produced through muscular work) accumulation will be delayed, thus preserving energy stores to some extent. It also stalls the buildup of lactic acid—the culprit that often puts a stop to muscular work. In essence, the rise in temperature allows you to do more work without becoming fatigued.

Higher temperatures within a muscle also improve nerve-muscle interaction. The transmission of nerve impulses to and from the muscles is more rapid following warm-ups and increased tempera-

Exercises and The Body Parts Each Affects Most

Partial List of Exercises	Anatomical Location	Primary Muscle(s) Affected and Movements Produced
1. Squat	Upper legs	Quadriceps (straightens leg) Hamstrings (bends leg)
2. Leg press	Upper legs	Quadriceps (as above) Hamstrings (as above)
3. Leg extension	Front thigh	Quadriceps (straightens leg)
4. Leg curl	Rear thigh	Hamstrings (bends leg)
5. Stiff-leg deadlift (back arched)	Rear thigh	Hamstrings (as above)
6. Bench press	Chest	Pectorals (moves elbows together before body)
7. Dumbbell bench press	Chest	Pectorals (as above)
8. Flye	Chest	Pectorals (as above)
9. Pec deck	Chest	Pectorals (as above)
10. Crossover	Chest	Pectorals (as above)
11. Chest dips	Chest	Pectorals (as above)
12. Overhead press	Front shoulders	Anterior deltoid (raises elbows upward before body)
13. Front deltoid raise	Front shoulders	Anterior deltoid (as above)
14. Lateral raise	Outside shoulders	Medial deltoid (raises shoulder outward)
15. Upright row	Outside shoulders	Medial deltoid (as above)
16. Bent-over lateral raise	Rear shoulders	Posterior deltoid (moves elbows to rear)
17. Shoulder shrugs	Neck/ shoulders	Trapezius (raises shoulders)
18. Reverse-grip pulldown	Upper sides, back	Latissimus dorsi (lowers elbows and moves arms to rear)
19. Pulldown	Upper sides, back	Latissimus dorsi (as above)
20. Chin-ups	Upper sides, back	Latissimus dorsi (as above)
21. Pull-ups	Upper sides, back	Latissimus dorsi (as above)
22. Seated row	Upper back	Latissimus dorsi (as above)
23. Stiff-leg deadlift (back rounded)	Lower back	Spinal erectors (extends torso)
24. "Good mornings"	Lower back	Spinal erectors (as above)
25. Pushdown	Rear upper arms	Triceps (straightens arm)
26. Close-grip bench press	Rear upper arms	Triceps (as above)
27. Seated French curl	Rear upper arms	Triceps (as above)
28. Lying French curl	Rear upper arms	Triceps (as above)
29. Tricep dips	Rear upper arms	Triceps (as above)
30. Standing bicep curl	Front upper arm	Biceps (bends arm)
31. Dumbbell curl	Front upper arm	Biceps (bends arm)
32. Preacher curl	Front upper arm	Biceps (as above)
33. Hammer curl	Front upper arm, Outside forearm	Biceps, forearm Extensors
34. Reverse curl	Front upper arm, Outside forearm	Biceps, forearm Extensors (as above, extends wrist)
35. Standing calf raise	Rear lower leg	Gastrocnemius (moves forefoot downward)
36. Seated calf raise	Rear lower leg	Soleus (as above)
37. Wrist curl	Inside forearm	Forearm flexors (bends wrist inward)
38. Reverse crunch	Lower midsection	Lower abdominals (bends spine forward)
39. Knee-up	Lower midsection	Lower abdominals (as above)
40. Twisting crunch	Midsection sides	Obliques (rotates torso)
41. Roman chair crunch	Upper midsection	Upper abdominals (bends spine forward)
42. Incline crunch	Upper midsection	Upper abdominals (as above)
43. Rope pull	Upper midsection	Upper abdominals (as above)

tures. This alone might be important during a racer's preparation for a race. Warm-ups are essential to the control of intricate movements on the racetrack and in the gym.

As your body heats up, articular surfaces within the joints (ends of the bones) increase in cartilage thickness. This will help ensure smooth and relatively friction-free movement. According to research work done by Inglemark and Ekholm (1949), such cartilage can increase 12-13 percent in thickness within ten minutes.

Elevated muscular temperatures also stimulate vasodilation (increase in blood vessel size). This enables your circulatory system to more efficiently deliver necessary substances to the working muscles, along with removing waste products from them.

In fact, blood distribution gradually shifts during warm-ups. Additional flow to the muscles is facilitated, and flow to the organs in your abdominal cavity (such as your stomach) decreases. This means greater cardiac output (blood flow from your heart) is directed to your skeletal muscles to provide energy for more intense muscular work.

All of these changes occur or should occur during your warm-ups. As you can see, warming up prepares you to get the most out of your strength training as well as your motorsports performance. The warm-up chart illustrates the three main categories of warm-ups, and shows how they affect your strength training performance.

These warm-up techniques are unlikely to be beneficial for a driver before a race, but may contribute to improved performance of the pit crew during pit stops.

Although specific to the individual and the activity, warm-ups should consist of at least five minutes of low-intensity work. Of course the more fit you are, the more you need to sufficiently warm

up. This is due in part to a well-conditioned person's thermoregulatory system becoming more efficient in response to heat production during physical work. Thus, a more intense and/or longer warm-up is necessary to elevate intramuscular temperatures in the fit individual.

But remember, your warm-ups cannot be *too* intense or they will impose on your energy demands needed for quality performance. If you exercise in a cold room, you must warm up adequately so that you overcome that already lower body temperature. This can be somewhat counteracted with appropriate workout clothing.

To some, light sweating indicates an adequate warm-up. But to be more scientific, you need to elevate your intramuscular temperatures 2-3 degrees (deg) Celsius. This usually takes a minimum of five minutes. Pre-race warm-up recommendations are included later in the chapter.

5.3 The Importance of Stretching

Even though muscle temperature may seem to be of greatest concern when it comes to warm-ups, muscle "looseness" or flexibility is also essential to safety and productivity. Not only does a muscle produce more force when it is stretched before being contracted, but a reduced risk of joint injury is evident when tissues possess more elastic qualities. In particular, the risk of injury is lowered when muscles, tendons, and ligaments are strong in a complete range of motion.

When muscles experience a rise in temperature they also experience a concomitant increase in blood flow. Since muscles that have a high blood saturation tend to be more elastic in nature, higher blood flow into a specific area will undoubtedly reduce the chances of injury during exercise as well as during motorsports activities.

Including stretching in your warm-up program

Value of Various Warm-up Techniques			
Warm-up Technique	Advantage	Disadvantage	Benefits for Strength Training
Passive (sauna, steam) (outside means)	Reduced chances of depleting energy stores	Directs blood flow to the skin rather than to the muscles	Marginal
General (calisthenics)	Increases overall body temperature	Directs blood flow to body's core, not to specific muscles	OK during initial stages of warm-ups
Specific (a beginning set of higher repetitions using light weight)	Concentrates on increasing the temperatures of specific muscles, improves muscle elasticity, acts as arehearsal for work sets of exercises	If strenuous, will hinder performance	Done at low to moderate intensity prior to more intense work sets

53

Stretching Techniques and Potential Problems

Stretching Techniques	Characterized by	Associated Problems
Ballistic *(pulling against tissues)*	Forceful movements that place undue stress primarily on the muscles and tendons	Can produce tissue tearing
Static *(held for more than 6sec)*	Holding of a stretched position to allow for tissue extension	Can produce tissue tearing if stretch is taken too far
PNF *(10sec contraction/ 10sec relaxation)*	Lower force muscle contractions performed while in a stretched position to allow for greater tissue elasticity during the relaxation phase effort	Can produce tissue tearing if the muscle contraction is greater than 40 percent

not only contributes to higher muscular capabilities, it also increases the elasticity of your tendons, ligaments, and other connective tissues. This can be accomplished during your specific warm-up set that is performed with light weights and high repetitions. Just be sure to carry each warm-up repetition through a complete range of motion.

When you stretch properly you should feel a tightness in the muscles being stretched, that diminishes within 5-6sec. If you force your muscles beyond that point, you'll be on your way to muscle, tendon, or ligament damage.

There are two basic categories of stretching: ballistic and static. Ballistic stretching consists of a series of "pulls" against resistant tissues; for instance, when you perform a bouncing effect during a calf raise when your heels are lowered toward the floor. This places undue stress on your Achilles tendon and the gastrocnemius muscle itself. Stretching in this manner can be dangerous and should be dropped from your routine.

Static stretching, on the other hand, relies on holding a stretched position for at least 7sec. This will allow the muscles, tendons, and connective tissues to gradually increase their own elasticity. We recommend that you pause in the stretched position for about 10sec, release the stretch, and then repeat as many times as necessary.

Another more advanced means of stretching is known as Proprioceptive Neuromuscular Facilitation (PNF). This approach includes techniques like hold-relax, contract-relax, and partner-assisted stretching.

For a better understanding of PNF stretching, let's look at partner-assisted stretching for your lower back. Sit on the floor with your legs straight out in front of you. You can keep your legs slightly bent so your hamstring muscles don't come into play here. Your partner places his or her hands on your middle to upper back and *very slowly* pushes your chest toward your knees, until your lower back muscles tighten. At this point, your partner holds you in that position while you attempt to lower your back to the floor.

A word of caution: You should not attempt this by using more than roughly 40 percent of the strength of your lower back muscles.

As this lower force muscle contraction is held for nearly 10sec, your muscles and tendons gradually stretch out. Then relax and repeat as necessary. Most PNF techniques incorporate a 10sec effort phase (some type of muscle contraction) and a similar relaxing phase.

Although PNF techniques are capable of producing the greatest increase in flexibility of a joint, a partner is almost always needed. This tends to be costly time-wise and takes more knowledge to properly institute.

The accompanying table lists the three basic techniques for stretching, and how each can produce injury when done improperly.

As illustrated, stretching can be harmful if not performed correctly. By no means should ballistic stretching replace stretching done in a static manner.

Chapter 7 describes some stretches that will improve your joint flexibility and perhaps contribute to recovery from exercise. In addition, many of these stretches are beneficial during rehabilitation of injured body parts.

5.4 How Many Reps?

A repetition is one complete movement. Take the bicep curl for example. A repetition is when you completely raise, then lower the weight.

When you begin any type of progressive resistance training (such as strength training), your repetitions should be moderately high. This requires you to use lighter weights, thus producing less unfamiliar stress on the tissues of your body (such as the muscles and tendons). Depending on your overall physical condition and lifestyle, you should continue with such general conditioning for four to eight weeks. The better shape you are in to start with and the more active your lifestyle, the less time you'll need for general conditioning.

For general conditioning for males we recommend a range of eight to twelve repetitions for most exercises. For females, the range is ten to fifteen. The exceptions to these repetition ranges are exercises designed to strengthen the gastrocnemius (calves) and the abdominal muscles. Since these muscles are predominantly comprised of slow-twitch fibers that are endurance oriented, they must be trained accordingly. That will require anywhere between the range of fifteen to twenty repetitions per set.

To improve your aerobic or cardiovascular function, you must follow a program of circuit training. The repetition requirements are the same as for general conditioning. The only variable is the rest time between sets and exercises. This is discussed in greater detail later in the chapter.

When the actual strength training regimen is begun, the resistance is raised and the repetitions lowered. Improvement in strength is best obtained within a six to eight repetition range. This means the weight should be increased when eight repetitions are performed in strict form within a single set. If six repetitions are not possible (in strict form), the weight being used is too heavy.

To increase speed and power, a minimum of two and not more than five repetitions must be performed . This requires a high number of muscle motor units (nerves stimulating muscle fibers to contract) which in turn produces a high output of force. This is power. And power is what's needed for fast, forceful movements like those required for speed.

Muscle enlargement or hypertrophy is a result of structural changes within the muscle cells themselves. Included among these changes are the increases in contractile proteins within the cells, along with additional storage of water and glycogen (carbohydrates). There are numerous scientific studies proving the enlargement of already existing cells as a result of strength training. However, controversy exists regarding the actual increase in the number of muscle cells (hyperplasia). It is possible that the number of cells increase through activation of satellite cell development. Satellite cells are existing cells that have previously not been developed.

The muscle fibers (cells) vary within your muscles. Although almost every muscle has some fast-twitch fibers and some slow-twitch fibers, it is the fast-twitch that you should be most concerned with. These are the fibers that enlarge the most and produce the greatest force output. In essence, they are the muscle fibers responsible for most of your driving duties.

We recommend a range of eight to ten repetitions per set for muscle hypertrophy of the fast-twitch muscle fibers. Again, the exceptions are calf and abdominal exercises. To enlarge the slow-twitch muscle fibers, we recommend a range of fifteen to forty repetitions per set.

Rehabilitation dictates similar repetition requirements. During initial rehabilitation when resistance is required, repetitions ranging from fifteen to forty are highly suggested. This range improves blood flow to injured tissues through the stimulation of slow-twitch muscle fibers that already have a high blood supply. This enhances recovery.

The accompanying chart illustrates the various repetition ranges dictated by specific goals.

Although your goals dictate your repetition ranges for each exercise, keep in mind that you should not follow the same strength training program for more than eight to twelve weeks. This can lead to overtraining. You must gear (cycle) your program so you are your strongest at the start of your racing season. And gauge your training to maintain as much strength as possible throughout the season.

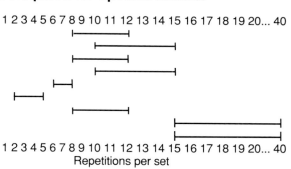

Repetition Ranges Required for Specific Results

General condition–Males
General condition–Females
Circuit training–Males
Circuit training–Females
Strength training
Power/speed
Muscle hypertrophy (fast-twitch fibers)
Muscle hypertrophy (slow-twitch fibers)
Initial resistance training rehabilitation

1 2 3 4 5 6 7 8 9 10 11 12 13 14 15 16 17 18 19 20 ... 40
Repetitions per set

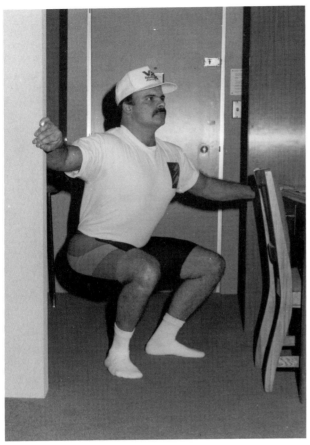 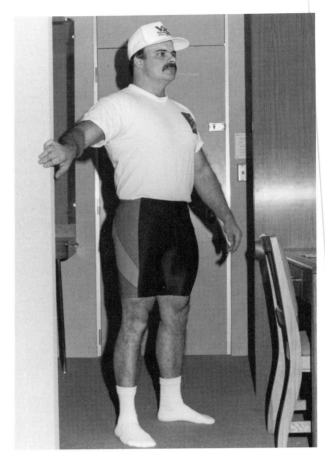

Full body squat: In a shoulder-width stance, with toes pointed outward slightly, slowly squat down until your upper legs are parallel to the floor (first photo). Then rise (second photo) and repeat until your upper leg muscles become fatigued. You'll likely know when this occurs be- *cause your quadriceps (front thigh muscles) will feel like they are burning. One or two sets until failure will suffice. It might be wise to hold on to something stable in case you lose your balance throughout the movement.*

5.5 How Many Sets?

Once again, your goals, time availability, and exercise tolerance help to determine the number of sets per exercise you should perform. A set is a series of repetitions performed in succession.

Although we highly recommend strengthening all of your major muscle groups, you should place an emphasis on those most involved in your racing duties. The requirements for the driver differ from those on the pit crew.

You certainly can benefit from performing one set of each exercise to the point of momentary muscular failure; however, benefits are increased by doing more. Three sets of an exercise, each carried to failure, is ideal. Muscular failure refers to the point at which you cannot perform another additional repetition in good strict form.

When time is limited or tolerance to exercise is low, it is wise to perform a single set of most exercises and two to three sets of each exercise most affecting your problem areas. For instance, if you ex-perience fatigue in your shoulders while racing, you might perform three sets of each exercise affecting these muscles while performing only one set each of the other exercises.

But keep in mind, more is not always better. Quality is the most important factor affecting your exercise results. It is better to do less—but do it intensely—than to waste time performing multiple sets that are easy.

When time is available and your interest high, three sets of each exercise will provide you with the maximum benefits. You'll also improve your strength endurance by increasing your training volume to this level. This increases your ability to repeat maximal force output, time after time without any appreciable reduction in strength.

5.6 Training Intensity

The degree of intensity at which you train is perhaps the most important ingredient of strength training success.

Push-ups: Position yourself between two stable objects (a bed or chair, for example), with the objects located slightly more than shoulder width apart. With your feet anchored on a chair or bed located between the stable objects (to provide additional resistance) and hands posi-tioned at chest (not shoulder) level, slowly lower your upper body between the stable objects as far down as possible (first photo). Then rise to complete arms' length (second photo). Repeat as many times as possible. One or two sets of this exercise will do the trick.

 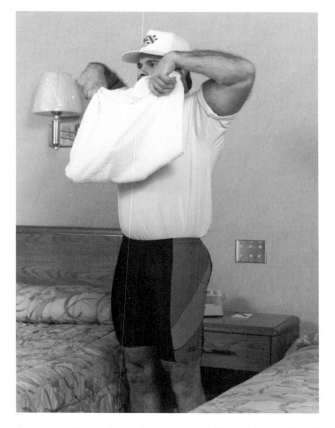

Upright row: In each hand, grasp a towel filled with ash trays, shoes, or anything that can provide weight. Begin with your arms fully extended downward against your thighs (first photo). Slowly raise your elbows upward until your hands reach shoulder level (second photo). Then lower to full arms' length and repeat. Note: Always "lead" with your elbows. Never allow your wrists to rise higher than your elbows. And keep the towel close to your body at all times throughout the movement. Do as many as you can for one or two sets.

57

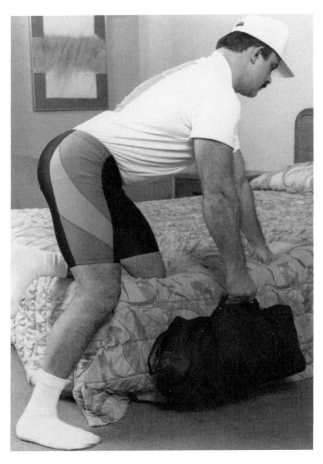

One-arm row: Kneel on a bed or chair with one knee and balance yourself by placing your hand on the same side, onto the supporting object. Flatten or slightly arch your back. Place your other leg about 1 or 2ft to the side of the supporting object. Grasp the handle of a gym bag with your free hand. Fully extend your arm that's holding the bag downward (first photo) and, leading with your el-

bow, raise the bag as far as possible while keeping your arm close to your body (second photo). Lower completely, then repeat as many times as possible. To increase resistance, simply fill the gym bag with shoes, ashtrays, or any other weighty objects available in your room. One or two sets to failure is recommended.

You get out of your exercise (benefits) what you put into your training (effort). It's like racing: The more intensely you drive, the greater your chances of winning. Regardless, you must train at a minimum level in order to benefit by becoming stronger, faster, and more flexible, and subsequently more capable as a driver or crew member.

Surprising to some, you needn't feel completely drained when you have completed your workout. On the other hand, if you don't work hard enough, your benefits are minimal. By carrying each set of repetitions to momentary muscular failure, you maximize your benefits and utilize your training time most efficiently.

Of course, it is impossible for anyone to work at a high intensity all the time. Such is the basis for periodization, also called cycle training. This simply means you train hard for a period to attain some short-range goals. Then as you become bored

or simply do not improve, you reduce your training effort. For example, you may concentrate on improving your bench press by following a programmed ten-week benching cycle or training program. As you reach your peak, your improvement just isn't there. This is a signal for change. Even if you were capable of training intensely year-round, it's likely that you would overtrain and increase your risks of injury.

There are ways of increasing your training intensity to the levels required for additional benefits. Let's take your biceps for example. With a goal of maximally improving bicep strength, you might include negative movements (eccentric contractions) one time each week during a ten-week bicep-emphasis program. You can do this by performing as many repetitions with a dumbbell (one arm at a time) as possible, then increase your training intensity by using your other hand to help raise the

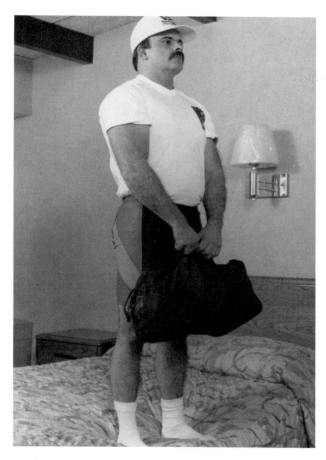

Back extension: Standing with feet slightly less than shoulder width apart, with toes forward and legs straight, grasp any object that will provide resistance (such as a small suitcase or a duffel bag containing weighty objects) in front of your body, at arms' length (first photo). The more you fill the bag the greater the resistance—you need this resistance. Slowly lower the bag toward the floor as far as possible keeping your legs straight. Pause in the lowered position for 2 or 3 seconds (second photo). Then rise to a standing position and repeat. One set to failure is sufficient. You may need to stand on a chair or dresser in order to complete a full range of motion—just be careful.

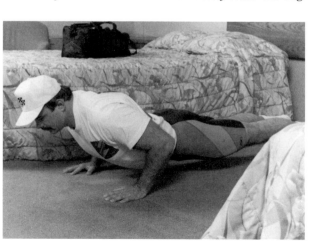

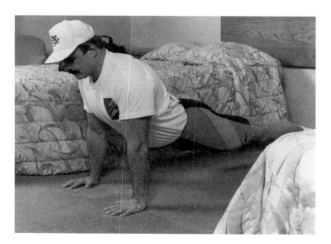

Tricep push-up: Facing the floor, place your hands on the floor with elbows resting slightly against your sides. Make sure your hands are located at lower chest level. Lower your chest to a point about 4in from the floor (first photo), then push your body upward until your arms are fully extended (second photo). Keep your elbows close to your body. Perform one or two sets in a slow, rhythmic manner until you cannot continue.

weight, then lower it only with the use of the already fatigued bicep until no additional negatives can be performed. This will be discussed later.

Because negatives and forced repetitions are strenuous for your muscles to perform, we recommend you perform them only once a week per muscle group. More often would be detrimental. It is likely that performing these "assisted" reps will increase muscle soreness. Research has shown an association between increased muscle soreness and eccentric muscle work and a subsequent need for longer recovery time.

With this in mind, you must realize that you cannot always improve. If you could, you'd likely see strength athletes carrying cars around on their shoulders. Your goal should be to become as strong as you can in order to be a better racer and to protect your body from injury. Unless your goal is to bench press 400lb or squat 600lb, there's no reason a racer needs to include this in his or her goals.

Using the rating scale shown in the accompanying table, you can determine for yourself how hard you must work to achieve the desired benefits. The information recorded is based on the appraisal of your own training efforts. Remember, you get out of it what you put into it.

However, it is important that most of your training be at a level with a subjective rating of at least 9-10. This means carrying each set of repetitions to momentary muscular failure. But, there is a time for training at lower ratings, and rehabilitation is one of those times.

Obviously, when you experience an injury, you lose some muscle function and sometimes a loss of strength or flexibility. Depending on the severity of the injury, your training level must be appropriate. If the injury is only slight (such as a small strain), your training intensity might be 5-8 on the perceived exertion scale. But if the injury is more severe (such as a fracture), then rehabilitation should begin at a level of 1-2, after casting is removed and range of motion is restored.

Even your warm-up sets should be at a lower level of effort than actual work sets. Your perceived exertion at this time should be roughly 5-6 with the use of lighter weights.

The accompanying table illustrates the various possible effort levels of strength training. The ratings reflect the strength trainer's psychological perception of the physical exertion achieved for a training period. The subjective ratings are a product of duration (repetitions performed) and the load (resistance used). As a progressive resistance program is undertaken, RPE-RT (Rate of Perceived Exertion—Resistance Training) decreases at a given workload (repetitions x load).

For instance, today you may rate your RPE-RT at 11 while performing eight repetitions with 150lb in the bench press, but as your training pro-

Rating of Perceived Exertion for Resistance Training (RPE-RT)

A psycho-physical scale for use in rating perceived exertion (effort) during resistance-type exercise

Subjective Rating	Subjective Analysis	Intensity Level	Implications For:
1-2 Very easy	Not strenuous at all	Low	Initial rehab phase I
3-4 Easy	Slight increase in ventilation (breathing)	Low	Rehab phase II
5-6 Moderate	Stop before reaching temporary muscular failure	Medium	Rehab phase III and Warmups
7-8 Somewhat hard	One additional repetition possible	Medium	Rehab phase IV and Off-cycle training
9-10 Hard	Not able to perform one more strict repetition	High	Improvment-oriented training
11-12 Very hard	Not able to perform one additional forced repetition	High	Goal-oriented training
13-14 Very very hard	Not able to perform one additional negative repetition (eccentric muscle contraction)	Very high	Occasional training techniques (1x/week)

gresses, say six weeks from now, this workload (repetitions x weight) gets easier and your RPE-RT may fall to 7. This simply means that you are getting stronger in that movement.

Through the experience of strength training, it becomes possible for you to effectively evaluate the effort you put forth during your exercise. By honestly "feeling" how hard you are working, you can determine what category your effort should fall into.

This rating helps you to determine what level of work is needed to accomplish your goals. Keep in mind that you need not always exercise at a level that leaves you feeling completely exhausted.

5.7 Speed of Movement

To *be* fast, you should *train* fast. Sounds simple, but it isn't. Although speedy movements are necessary in some racing situations, you should neither perform all repetitions in this manner nor train this way all the time. It's stressful to both your muscles and your tendons.

Bicep curl: Holding on to a duffel bag or anything that will provide ample resistance (15-40lb weights, for example) with two hands, slowly curl the object upward until your arms are completely flexed (first photo). Then slowly

lower your body until your arms are fully extended near your thighs (second photo) and repeat. Do this as many times as possible for one or two sets.

Always begin a general conditioning program (which precedes actual strength training) in a slow-repetition manner. This means about 2sec raising the weight, held for one second when the muscle is fully contracted, then lowering for roughly 3-4sec. This constitutes one repetition.

By performing your repetitions at a slower speed, you reduce the risk of injury to your muscles and tendons. Since your tendons often are the weak link in your muscle-tendon junction, the tendons usually get injured when repetitions are done in a fast manner. But this is likely to happen only when the tendons have not adapted properly to resistance training. Your tendons adapt by becoming stronger similar to the way your muscles get stronger. This is, in part, the basis of why general conditioning is needed before strength training is begun, and why strength is needed before speed-power training is undertaken.

Slow-repetition training is almost always recommended when training your calves (gastrocnemius) and your abdominals because these muscles contain predominantly slow-twitch muscle fibers. It is also recommended during rehabilitation so you don't place unnecessary stress on an injured muscle, tendon, or connective tissue while increasing blood flow to these tissues.

Going slower than the 2sec-1sec-4sec fashion may not be as beneficial due to the subsequent blood flow impairment. Impairment can occur when muscles remain tense or contracted for prolonged periods. Performing repetitions faster places the tendons connecting the muscles to bones and perhaps the muscles themselves at risk for tearing.

Muscle hypertrophy (enlargement) is best achieved through a slow-repetition style of training. In addition to protecting the soft tissues from injury, it also provides resistance throughout most of the movement. Slow repetition also alleviates any momentum from occurring throughout every repetition.

However, there are times when you need to raise the weight in a fast manner. This benefits

 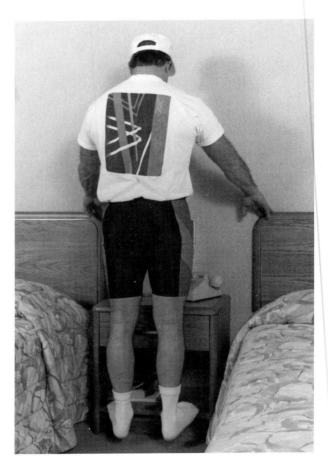

Calf raise: Supporting your body weight on the balls of your feet with heels hanging off a step, slowly raise your body by pushing the balls of your feet downward (first photo). Pause for 1sec, then lower your heels as far as possible (second photo) and again pause for 1sec. Do

these slowly and rhythmically until you cannot perform another repetition. One set of this exercise will suffice. If additional resistance is needed, perform each repetition with all weight supported by one foot. Maintain balance and support by holding on to an immovable object.

both speed and power. Since these two terms are synonymous when it comes to strength training, we'll simply define power. Power (P) is equal to force (strength; f in the formula) times distance (d) divided by time (t). The formula may look more familiar to you in this fashion:

$$P = (f \times d) / t$$

P = power
f = force or strength
t = time
d = distance

Since our muscles are predetermined in their possible ranges of motion, distance is constant. By simply substituting strength for force, we end up with the formula:

$$P = s / t$$

P = power
s = strength
t = time

As you can see by the revised formula, strength is a prerequisite for power and when you

are concerned with speed and power, you are also concerned with fast, forceful repetitions.

Fast movements are needed in several situations involving racing pit crews. For instance, a pit crew member may need to get to the race vehicle quickly to perform his duties in a timely fashion, then quickly return to the pit wall.

As previously stated, to be fast you need to train fast. In a majority of instances, this only applies to raising the weight. Most often you should maintain control of the weight when lowering it, which again means a 3-4sec lowering of the weight. However, there is one basic exception to this rule, and this occurs while performing plyometrics. Plyometrics will be discussed later in the chapter.

5.8 Rest Time Between Sets and Exercises

The rest intervals between sets and exercises depends mostly on how rapidly you recover from the work intervals (previous sets), as well as how intensely you train. Through the conditioning process of becoming stronger, your body improves its ability to recover from these work periods. It then takes less time for you to be prepared for the following sets and exercises.

The more intensely you work out, the longer it takes your body to remove waste products resulting from exercise while replenishing energy stores. Since strength and power training affects primarily your fast-twitch muscle fibers, additional rest time is needed for adequate recovery of these muscle cells before work can again be performed with sufficient force output. Remember, these muscle fibers receive less blood flow than slow-twitch fibers and thus require more time for recovery.

Therefore, the heavier and more intense your training, the longer the rest period between sets and exercises. During high-repetition, slow-movement exercise like that during rehabilitation, it is the slow-twitch muscle fibers that are being affected. As a result, rest between sets and exercises is often of less duration.

There is a means of enhancing this recovery between work intervals known as active rest. Active rest refers to performance of easier, more passive work between sets of exercises. This passive rest can be comprised of moderate walking, abdominal exercises, or calf raises. Although each of these exercises stimulates muscular activity, the muscles affected are of predominantly slow-twitch fibers, and thus recover quickly. This can help save time during workouts, and promotes recovery of other more intensely worked muscles.

Another way to save time working out is to alternate exercises for separate body parts. For example: Following a set of repetitions in the bicep curl, you can proceed (in less than 30sec) to the calf raise. Then you repeat this sequence as many times as necessary to complete your predetermined number of sets per exercise.

The accompanying table illustrates the various recommended rest periods between sets and exercises, which are determined in part by the type of training you are following. Your goals dictate the type of training you perform.

5.9 Training Formats and Rest Time Recommendations

Training Format	Recommended Rest Time
General conditioning	1-2min
Circuit training	15-30sec
Strength training	1-3min
Power-speed training	3-5min
Muscle hypertrophy (fast-twitch fibers)	2-3min
Muscle hypertrophy (slow-twitch fibers)	30sec-1min
Rehabilitation	30sec-1min

The table shows how much time should be taken between sets and between exercises during resistance training. As you can see, less rest is needed when slow-twitch muscle fibers are predominantly used during any given exercise format.

Looking at the recommended rest periods, you can see that each rest period is represented within a range of time. As you become better conditioned in any of the training formats, your body becomes more capable of recovering more quickly. It might

Crunch: Lie on your back with your hands crossed over your chest, heels near your buttocks, and chin tucked (first photo). Slowly curl your shoulders up and off the floor as far as possible without raising your lower back *off the floor (second photo). Push your lower back downward against the floor. Repeat this movement as many times as possible for one set.*

be wise to begin your specific training regimen by utilizing the longest of the time period range recommended for your rest periods and as you progress, lower your rest period to the minimum time allowed within the range. Be cautious, however, not to leave any less time between sets than the minimum recommendations.

The Importance of Stretching

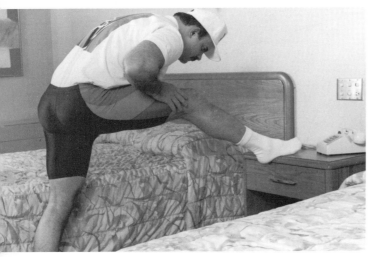

Hamstring stretch: In addition to the suggested exercises shown in this chapter, we strongly advise selected stretches to maintain flexibility of the joints most involved in racing performance. We'll start with the hamstring stretch. With knee bent, place your foot on a chair or bed and lean forward as far as possible. Place your opposite foot about 4-5ft behind you and keep the knee slightly bent (first photo). Remain leaning forward as you gently straighten your forward leg until your hamstring muscle tightens (second photo). Pause for nearly 10sec, then again bend the knee and move forward. Repeat this procedure with each leg, four to five times. For best results, keep your back arched.

5.10 Workout Frequency

You know how many sets and how many reps you need to build your body, but you may be somewhat confused about how many times a week you should train a particular muscle or muscle group.

There is limited scientific information available on the subject. However, there are some physiological guidelines that can help you determine the recovery you need between workouts of the same muscle group.

The scientific literature that is available on the subject indicates a proven need for recovery. Without adequate recovery from strenuous workouts, your muscles will take a break themselves. When this happens, you will become stale, fail to improve, experience declining performance, and possibly become injured.

It is known that not all muscle groups require the same recuperation period. For instance, muscles of slow-twitch fiber predominance require less time for full recovery than fast-twitch fiber muscles. This is due to the high volume of blood flowing to the slow-twitch fibers.

It doesn't take a scientist to know that:

1. Without strenuous, high-intensity workouts, you cannot stimulate muscles to grow; and

2. Without sufficient recovery from your strenuous workouts, you won't allow your muscles to adapt by becoming stronger and more powerful.

Whenever you have experienced complete recovery between workouts, you feel great and usu-

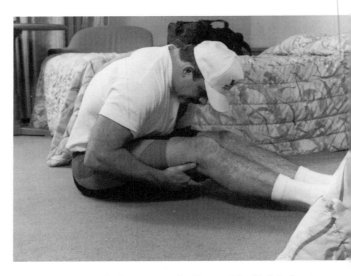

Lower back stretch: Sitting on the floor with slightly bent knees, grasp the underside of your legs with your hands and lean forward. You can use your hands to help pull your chest toward your knees, but don't overdo it. Lean forward until your lower back muscles tighten up, and pause in the position for 10sec. Sit straight up then repeat four to five times. Make sure to "round out" your back, don't keep it arched.

ally have no problem lifting heavier weights or doing one or two more repetitions than you did in past workouts. Just think, if you could do this every time you train a lift, you could very likely do better than ever before. But we all have present-day potentials. That is, we progress only so much before we hit a plateau in performance (possible overtraining) and find it virtually impossible to improve. The key to strength training success is to approach overtraining without undertraining. You do this by permitting complete recovery between workouts of the same muscle groups.

When you train for strength, your muscles become fatigued, mainly from energy deficiency and neuromuscular impairment. Fatigued muscles become drained of adenosine triphosphate (ATP), the basic form of energy for muscular contraction. As you fatigue muscles, ATP stores within these muscles become drained and creatine phosphate (CP), another form of the muscle cell's energy fuel, is broken down to form additional ATP. As you already know, it doesn't take long for your muscles to become drained of these two energy stores. To fully recover from this hard work, these energy substrates (chemical compounds) must be completely replenished.

When ATP and CP stores are drained, glycogen is broken down to form additional CP. Glycogen stores in the muscles and liver, and hence must be replaced during recovery. This is done through the consumption of carbohydrates. Glycogen, the energy that is utilized by the working muscles during resistance training, also becomes drained. Glycogen stores within the muscles and liver are used up as energy for your training session and also need to be replaced.

Pronounced fatigue has a detrimental effect on nerve-muscle interactions. There is an actual tearing of cellular structures responsible for carrying electrical impulses to the muscle; these impulses direct the muscle to contract. Due to the tearing, the impulses become weaker. This results in weaker contractions. Recovery allows a healing process to take place, thus enabling function of this electrical system again during the following workout of these muscles.

High-intensity training also produces microtrauma to various tissues. This is most notable following eccentric contraction movements, when the muscle tissue is forced to lengthen under tension. Minute tearing of the connective tissue results, producing the all-too-familiar feeling of muscle soreness.

So as you can see, strength training results in a host of damaging effects to your muscles and their electrical network. The more intense your training, the more damage is done.

To understand the major factors affecting muscle recovery, refer to the recovery time chart. Of utmost concern are your training intensity (how hard you train) and training volume (how much you do). Because you cannot train at a high intensity all year long, adjustments must be made not only in your training format, but also in your respective recovery periods.

Since we have established several factors affecting full recovery, and with full recovery being essential for building strong and powerful muscles, you should realize the importance of carefully planning your workouts. But first, we must establish some guidelines for how much time each muscle or muscle group needs to fully recover after stimulation, via resistance training.

The accompanying table illustrates some general guidelines for recovery, based on the most influential factor—training intensity—with all other factors considered as well. Recommendations can be adjusted to meet your particular needs and this table's information should be used only as a general guideline to help you be more productive in your training.

Chest stretch: Position yourself in a doorway. Place your hands on the doorjamb at low-chest level. Gently lean forward until your chest and/or shoulders tighten. Pause for 10sec, then step backward and relax. Repeat this four to five times.

Failure to allow a muscle to fully recover from a past workout is undeniably detrimental to optimal strength gains. And since guidelines have been set up to help determine the length of rest (per muscle group), you can structure your workouts accordingly. However, actual training experience, along with understanding all the factors affecting recovery, may give you the best idea of your own recovery ability.

5.11 When to Increase Resistance

To get the most benefits from strength training, you must attempt to do better than ever before. This can mean an increase in the number of repetitions you perform in a particular exercise with a given weight, or an increase in the weight you are using in any exercise.

While performing the maximum number of repetitions recommended for a specific training format (such as general conditioning) and using the same weights workout after workout, your body gets stale. It doesn't improve by becoming stronger. In fact, the workload gets easier for your muscles to handle, forcing these muscles to shift into a deconditioning mode. That is, your muscles are not stressed sufficiently and therefore don't adapt by becoming stronger.

The whole idea behind any type of resistance training is *progressive* resistance. This means ei-

Days Required to Fully Recover from Strength Training

Muscle(s)	>19 Reps / Set Low Intensity	8-12 Reps / Set Moderate Intensity	3-6 Reps / Set High Intensity
Neck	1 day	1.5 days	2 days
Chest	2	3	4
Shoulders	2	2.5	3
Upper back	2	3	4
Lower back	3	4	5
Midsection	1	1.5	2
Hips	3	3.5	4
Quadriceps	3	3.5	4
Hamstrings	3	3.5	4
Calves	1	1.5	2
Biceps	2	2.5	3
Triceps	2	2.5	3
Forearms	1	1.5	2

Source: Adapted from the *Complete Guide to Fitness Training,* International Sports Sciences Association, 1991, with permission granted from Fred Hatfield, Ph. D., director.

Major Factors Affecting Muscle Recovery

There are numerous concerns affecting your requirements for full recovery. By taking each factor into consideration, you can determine for yourself how long you must wait before resuming training of a particular muscle or muscle group. Below are some of these factors and how each affects recovery.

Training intensity: The higher the intensity, the longer it takes to fully recover. High intensity equals weights of 80 percent or greater, of one-rep maximum, carried to momentary muscular failure.

Forced reps and negatives increase intensity levels.

Training volume: The more you do, the longer your muscles need to fully recover. Obviously, doing nine sets per body part requires longer recovery than three sets per body part.

Muscle size: Larger muscles require longer recovery periods. That's why you should not train most of your muscles more than two or three times a week.

Range of motion: Larger range of motion exercises are more stressful on your muscles and tendons and require additional recovery time. This is the case with most dumbbell exercises. Partial movements recover faster.

Nutrition: Your tissues require carbohydrates to refill used-up energy stores and quality protein for the rebuilding process. This is of particular concern to those attempting to gain or lose weight.

Age: Research has shown that you can gain muscle strength at almost any age. However, aging increases the body's need for recuperation time. The older you are, the longer it takes to fully recover.

Therapeutic aids: The proper applications of ice, heat, whirlpool treatments, massage, and ultrasound can improve recovery by increasing blood flow and limiting swelling following exhaustive exercise. Ice should be applied to respective body parts following exercise and deep-tissue massage.

Sleep: Since your muscles recover while you sleep, it is essential that you get regular, noninterrupted sleep. Seven to nine hours nightly should suffice. A mid-afternoon nap can also help.

Stress: The more stress you have, the longer your recovery time. Remember, stress places some physiological demands on your body.

Aerobic training: An efficient cardiovascular system has increased blood-flow potential to your tissues, whereby allowing for faster removal of waste products and delivery of nutrients to your worked muscles. Circuit training can be an effective means of aerobic conditioning.

Stretching: Stretching your muscles and tendons helps increase blood flow to these tissues and helps to relax them during recovery times.

ther a gradual increase in resistance (weight), or an increase in the times you lift a weight (repetitions) as your muscles become stronger. If you neglect to stress your tissues sufficiently, you will not increase your strength.

Whenever you can perform the maximum number of repetitions (already determined in the table), you should increase the weight in a particular exercise approximately 5 to 10 percent. Generally speaking, you can raise the resistance 5 percent in exercises involving smaller muscles (such as bicep curls and tricep extensions), and 10 percent in those involving larger muscles (squats and bench presses).

However, if you raise the weight you are using in any exercise without being able to perform the minimum number of repetitions recommended, then you raised the weight too much. You'll need to lower it some.

For example: Let's say you can perform eight repetitions in the bench press, all in strict form, with 200lb. We'll say you are involved in an actual strength training regimen that requires you to perform six to eight repetitions per set. This should be a signal to you that the weight is too light. It may not seem light to you, especially if you busted a gut getting all eight repetitions. However, you should raise the weight for the following bench press workout. By raising the weight 20lb (10 percent), you might then perform only five repetitions. That is lower than the minimum recommendations of six reps. Therefore you are required to lower the weight, perhaps by 10lb. You should then be able to perform six or seven repetitions. This is OK, because you are within the desired range of repetitions.

The same scenario can be used for every exercise. Just remember, if you cannot perform the

Guidelines for Strength Training

Although each type of training—whether it be general conditioning, strength training, or power and speed training—has specific procedures to follow, all have similar guidelines. That is, specific rules you must adhere to for best results.

There are basically eleven rules to guide you in your strength training endeavor:

1. Warm up before you begin any exercise. This prepares your tissues for the more intense workloads ahead. Included are stretching and actual warm-up sets performed with light weights.

2. Know how many repetitions you are expected to perform. By looking at the table, you can determine the range of repetitions you should fall within for best results. Since you should reach momentary muscular failure in most of your sets of repetitions (excluding warm-ups), this helps you determine how much weight to use.

3. Perform your repetitions at a speed that has been established for each type of strength training. Every repetition should be performed slowly unless you are involved in power and speed training which utilizes fast, forceful repetitions. The lowering phase of every repetition, regardless of your training format, should be performed in a slower, more controlled manner.

4. All repetitions should be performed in strict form. Cheating a weight upward only increases your risk of injury.

5. Utilize a complete range of motion whenever possible. Each muscle group should be stressed in the extreme ranges of motion, especially in the stretched position. This increases your joint flexibility and more importantly, your strength in the extreme ranges of motion.

6. Workouts should always begin with the largest muscle groups first, then proceed down the line to the smaller, more isolated muscles. This means training your chest, legs, and back before your arms and calves, thus alleviating a smaller muscle becoming the weak link while assisting in a larger muscle group exercise.

7. Variety is the spice of life. Variety is also the spice of exercise. Vary your workouts whenever you become bored. This helps to maintain interest in what you are doing.

8. Make sure you stress all the major muscle groups of your body. Additional muscles involved in specific motorsports activities should be included.

9. Your results from strength training are based mainly on the training intensity by which you work. Keep in mind that the harder you work, the greater the benefits. Refer to the table to determine which intensity you should train at, in order to receive appropriate benefits. Remember, though, you cannot train at high intensities for long periods.

10. To guarantee recovery between sets, exercises, and workouts, you must allow time for your muscles to rebuild by means of rest. The recovery time chart illustrates some general guidelines for required rest between workouts of the same muscle group.

11. For best results, the three major concerns of exercise must be carefully considered. These are: Muscular stimulation (to facilitate the adaptation process of becoming stronger); Nutrition (for recovery from exercise and for adequate energy); and Rest (for work and workout recovery and stress reduction).

minimum recommended repetitions, lower the weight some. But when you *can* perform the maximum number of recommended repetitions, *increase* it. Don't allow your body to become bored or stale.

5.12 Knowing How and When to Change Your Program

When you do become bored or simply do not improve in the exercises you are performing, it's time for change. Without changing the routine, you will be likely to skip workouts altogether, and this is a no-no! Regularity is the key to exercise success; therefore, you must maintain interest in what you are doing.

One aspect of strength training that is different from most other forms of exercise is the ability to vary your workouts. This can be done by simply changing the order in which you perform certain exercises, altering the exercises themselves, or changing the format.

Although you are somewhat limited in the order in which exercises should be performed (largest muscle group exercises first), you can modify it to an extent. For instance, you may want to perform your exercises in what's known as a pre-exhaustion sequence. That is when you fatigue a muscle in its primary movement, then immediately call upon it to assist in a secondary movement.

Take, for example, a pre-exhaustion workout for your chest muscles (pectorals). A pre-exhaustion sequence would have you performing flyes first (a primary movement of your pectorals), then going immediately to the bench press where your chest muscles would be assisted by your shoulders (anterior deltoids) and your triceps to raise the bar upward.

Pre-exhaustion sequences can be performed for several muscle groups. The various sequences are described in greater detail later in this chapter.

There are almost unlimited numbers of exercises that can be performed for each muscle group. The accompanying table illustrates some of these strength training alternatives. By performing a different exercise for a particular muscle group, your interest can be retained, at least until you again become bored or don't improve.

A lack of improvement might be a signal that you are prepared for more intense training. You can increase your intensity by incorporating "negatives" and "forced reps" into your workout regimen. These techniques also are explained later in the chapter. Sometimes an increase in training intensity leads to additional progress.

But when all else fails, perhaps it's time to change your training format. This can mean graduation to strength training from general conditioning or power-speed training from a strength train-

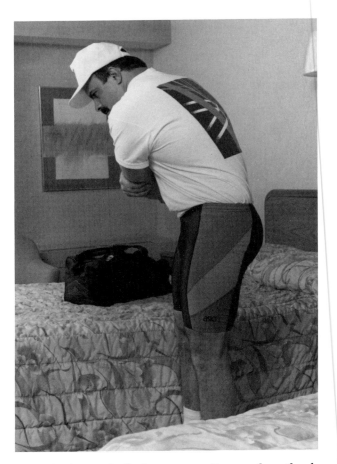

Upper back stretch: Grab your opposite arm above the elbow. Gently pull that arm toward the front and center of your body while you round your upper back. Move the arm across the front of your body until the muscles on that side of your upper back and shoulders tighten, pause for 10sec, then relax. Repeat this movement four to five times, then repeat with the other arm.

ing program. Hopefully, you can see how changes must be made in order to keep you working out.

We've said it once and we'll say it again: Variety is the spice of life—and variety is also the spice of exercise.

5.13 Guarding Against Overtraining

The physical demands associated with exercise disturb your body's homeostasis or, more simply, disrupt the normal stability of bodily functions. But don't worry, this is a natural occurrence. When this homeostasis becomes unstable or disrupted, your muscular strength decreases and you become fatigued easily. Often this occurs when a larger volume of training (for instance, with more than nine or ten sets per body part) is accompanied by high-intensity work. This results in a greater need for recovery time. Remember, the harder you work the longer it takes your body to

Glute stretch: Lying flat on the floor on your back with legs extended straight out, bend your right knee and place it over your left leg. Place your left hand on top of your upper right leg (just above the knee) and push *downward until your right buttock tightens. Hold for 10sec, relax, and repeat two more times. Then do the same for the other buttock.*

reestablish homeostasis; inadequate recovery results in overtraining.

A major concern in strength training is that you must overload your muscles to stimulate them to adapt by becoming stronger. By constantly trying to use more weight or do more repetitions, you will progress. But when the time comes that you have reached your present-day potential, further high-intensity training can lead to overtraining.

You will know when you reach this potential: you will feel more fatigued during your training periods and you will eventually experience a reduction in performance. You might do fewer reps with a particular weight, or have to lower your poundages in order to fulfill your repetition ranges. Your body is telling you to slow down. This is known as short-term overtraining. By cutting back on the intensity or duration of your workouts, you can help facilitate full recovery.

Physiologically, when you train in absence of full recovery, the motor units (nerve-muscle units that cause muscles to contract) that you usually recruit during an exercise will become premature-

ly fatigued. Your body therefore has to call upon additional motor units in order for you to successfully lift a particular load. This will cause your heart rate (pulse) and ventilation (breathing), among other things, to elevate.

If you experience such short-term overtraining, you might notice symptoms of increased fluid intake, abnormal sleep, and a possible reduction in body weight. Your racing performance will suffer as well, in the form of slower reaction times, feelings of lethargy, and frequent fatigue.

Long-term overtraining is frequently experienced by strength, physique, and speed athletes who commonly train at high intensities. It differs from short-term overtraining in that you virtually degrade your body for a longer period, and experience additional harmful effects such as increased heart rate, continual feelings of fatigue, decline in strength and muscular endurance, increased irritability, and loss of desire to train and perhaps race.

In addition, you may experience abnormal sleep patterns, loss of appetite, and a subsequent

Neck and shoulder stretch: Grasp hands in front of your body about chin level with arms fully extended. Reach out away from your body as far as possible until the muscles of your neck and/or upper shoulders tighten. Pause for 10sec, relax, and repeat three to five times as necessary. To stretch the neck muscles even more, gently glide your chin backward for the duration of the stretch. Do not tilt your head upward.

reduction in body weight. This is a point at which your body not only suggests full recovery—it *demands* it. Full recovery from such an overtraining syndrome has been known to take anywhere from a few weeks to six months. It depends on how long you have overtrained.

Because of the negative side effects accompanying long-term overtraining, it is not difficult to see why those who train hard for long periods become sick. This is due partially to a less effective immune system—another effect of long-term overtraining.

It is now believed that the intensity of your training is more crucial to possible overtraining than its duration. Although intensity is a major factor affecting exercise progress, it is agreed that long periods of intense training can be the groundwork for overtraining.

When any symptoms of overtraining are experienced, it's time for a change—either a new job or a new workout. Since your desire to be a better driver is evident by your reading this book, we will restrict our discussion to training. By identifying the signs of potential overtraining, you should make appropriate adjustments in your training (or lifestyle, if necessary) in order to accomplish your goals.

Overtraining is a means to an end. Racing enthusiasts who are highly motivated to succeed also tend to give 110 percent in most other things they do. They are individuals who are consequently more likely to experience overtraining syndrome, unless they are provided with good strength training information.

You can protect yourself from overtraining by ensuring that proper measures are taken. This means the right combination of training, rest, and smart nutritional habits. Training should be progressive in intensity and duration, rest should be of sufficient length and quality, and nutritional habits should be well balanced. In addition, your training should be cycled. You cannot train with heavy resistance and low repetitions at a high intensity yearlong.

When you return from a layoff, either following overtraining, racing commitments, or simply taking a break from training, workouts should be incremental in style. Begin training at a low to moderate intensity, together with fewer sets and exercises.

We have said it before and we'll say it again: It is better to undertrain slightly than to overtrain grossly. The chart illustrates several of the physical and mental factors that can cause overtraining.

5.14 Possible Causes of Overtraining
Physiological Causes
• Sudden increase in training loads
• Improper training practices
• Insufficient recovery
• Staleness in workout
• Doing too much too soon
• Monotonous training
• Not cycling training

Psychological Causes
• Job demands
• Motorsport demands
• Personal problems
• Fear of failure
• Environmental stress
• Training boredom
• Excessive goal setting

Be aware that these factors exist, and know how adjustments in strength training can be made to protect yourself from falling prey.

5.15 Promoting Recovery from Exercise
By now, you should be well aware that the three factors most affecting recovery from exercise are blood flow, nutrition, and rest. Without any one of these factors, your body will take longer to recover. This is true in racing, too. Just think how difficult it would be to race for 3-4 hours (hr) every day of the week. Within a few days, your body would be so fatigued, you could not possibly perform well.

Vertical jumps: Jump as high as you can ten times in a row with at least 15sec of rest between jumps. Your goal is to spend as little time on the ground and as much time in the air as possible. As you can see by the pictures, you begin by preparing to jump (first photo). Then, with the help of your arms, propel upward (second photo) and reach for the sky (third photo). One set, twice a week, will be adequate.

71

So it goes for improving your strength. If your muscles are not completely repaired before placing them again under the stress of training, your strength will not improve. In fact, without full recovery, your body is placed under more stress for prolonged periods, and your strength is likely to decline.

Here are six ways to guarantee faster recovery from exercise:

1. *You must be in good overall physical health.* This means an absence of illness and disease. When you are ill, your body has to work in overdrive to mend itself, resulting in a longer time for full recovery.

2. *You must have reasonably efficient heart and lung systems for effective central circulation.* When your heart is capable of pumping blood to working muscles without a large-scale sacrifice of blood flow to organs and other tissues, your body is more prepared for intense workloads without putting undue strain on your heart muscle. In addition, lung function must be adequate to supply oxygen to the bloodstream in absence of excessive heavy breathing. Together, your heart and lung function must be in good working order to facilitate nutrient rich blood to the tissues for faster recovery.

3. *You must have an efficient circulatory system supplying blood to the periphery of the body.* This refers to the arterial network providing blood flow to skeletal muscles. Recovery is enhanced by the increased size and number of vessels providing blood supply to the various muscles generated through strength training. There's no form of exercise other than resistance-type training that stimulates improved blood flow to so many of the major muscle groups of the body.

4. *You must control stresses of racing as well as those exerted by everyday living.* Undue stress restricts your body's ability to recover from exercise and illness. Strength training not only reduces stress levels through physical exertion, but it also increases psychological aspects of stress reduction through the likes of increased self-confidence and an improved sense of well-being.

Depth jumps: By stepping off an object, you place additional stress on your muscles to slow your downward movement when coming in contact with the floor. As you step off the object, think of spending as little time as possible on the floor (first photo). As you hit the floor, push off with your feet as hard as possible (second photo). Make sure your time in the air is longer than your time on the ground (third photo). Begin by using no more than a 12in object to step off from. You can work your way up to 36in, but caution is warranted—you'd better have a good foundation of strength first. Rest for no less than 15sec between jumps. One set of ten depth jumps is adequate.

5. *You must allow for adequate rest.* This not only refers to sound sleep, it also includes a little R&R (rest and relaxation) during strenuous, stressful daily activities. Be careful not to neglect appropriate recommendations for rest between workouts of the same muscle group. Inadequate rest impairs your body's ability to fully recover from strength training, as well as other physically and mentally demanding duties.

6. *You must maintain smart eating habits.* Of concern here is the consumption of complex carbohydrates, protein from quality sources, and a diet low in fat. In addition, five to six meals a day should be consumed. This permits the availability of nutrients required for repair and growth to be used by the body when it needs them.

There are additional techniques that can be used to promote recovery from intense exercise, but they may not always be practical due to time restraints. These practices include:

1. *You should alternate high-intensity (heavy day) workouts with moderate-intensity (light day) workouts.* Although you are benefiting from exercise during your moderate-intensity workouts, you are virtually enhancing your recovery from high-intensity exercise sessions. The higher repetitions involved in moderate-intensity workouts increase

blood flow to the working muscles, promoting recovery of these tissues.

2. *You should "listen" to your body.* If you feel tired or fatigued at the start of a workout, perhaps a day off is warranted. This may take some time to learn, but consciously evaluating how you feel can be a factor in allowing for complete recovery before exerting more stress on any given muscles through strength training.

3. *When time allows, you should massage strenuously worked muscles with ice immediately following a high-intensity workout.* This reduces swelling that naturally occurs as a result of intense training. Cryotherapy (the use of ice treatments) also contributes to a temporary increase in blood flow when the cold is removed. The body responds to a cooling effect (icing) by increasing blood supply to the local area. The result: an enhanced delivery of nutrients to the "damaged" muscles. *Caution:* Do not ice areas for more than ten to fifteen minutes. The lower your body fat of a particular body part, the shorter the icing time should be.

4. *You should use electrical muscle stimulation (EMS) to improve recovery through the increase in blood flow to the "connected" muscles.* Through proper use of EMS, your muscles become more relaxed while reducing the incidence of muscle spasms that sometimes occur following intense resistance exercise. Both benefits improve your ability to recover. *Caution:* Before using any electrical stimulation device, consult a qualified sports fitness expert.

5. *You should use heat to increase blood flow to your tissues as they increase in temperature.* Research shows that moist heat may be more productive than dry heat. You can do this by placing your dry heating pad on top of a dry towel which is placed above a moist towel. A moist towel warmed in a microwave is a viable alternative. Heat stimulates your blood vessels to dilate, thus increasing blood flow through these arteries and veins. Whatever your choice of heat, be careful not to burn your skin. *Note:* Do not apply heat treatments within 3-4hr after exercise.

6. *You should use massage as another means of promoting recovery from high-intensity strength training.* This not only helps to relax muscles, it temporarily increases blood flow: relaxation plus increased blood flow equals improved recovery. In addition, when deep sports massage is administered, adhesions resulting from heavy training are reduced in size. As a result, your muscles maintain their elasticity which in turn allows your muscles to produce more force output.

You should now have a better understanding of ways you can improve your recovery from any strength training format. Increased blood flow is a primary factor in reducing recovery time. Yet this is true only providing that your blood contains those essential nutrients required for tissue repair and growth. This can only be facilitated through smart eating.

5.16 Systems of Training

There are several methods you can use to achieve the desired benefits from strength training. The basic approach is the single-set format—performing one set of repetitions of an exercise, followed by a brief rest period, then a second set of repetitions, and so on. This can be very productive, especially when the set is carried to momentary muscular failure.

However, there are other training systems that can provide variety along with productivity. We have described nine of these systems below.

The first is *supersetting*. Supersetting simply means performing one set of an exercise immediately followed by another set of either the same exercise with a lesser weight; another exercise for the same muscle group; or an exercise for an opposing muscle or muscle group.

The first alternative is self-explanatory. The weight may need to be reduced anywhere from 10-50 percent, depending on how many repetitions you wish to successfully complete. And of course, the harder you work during the first set, the more you will need to reduce the weight for the second set.

The second option—another exercise for the same muscle group—contributes to an increased volume of work for a particular muscle or muscle group. Choosing this option, you may elect to perform a set of repetitions in the standing barbell curl immediately followed by a set of repetitions of preacher curls.

As for the third option, it's a real time-saver. Since reaching momentary muscular fatigue in one muscle group will not appreciably affect the work you do for an opposing muscle group, your training intensity can remain high in exercises for both muscle groups. This may be explained better by using upper arm training as an example. You can begin with a set of repetitions in the bicep curl, immediately followed by a set of repetitions of tricep pushdowns.

Because bicep curls will not prefatigue your tricep muscles, your training intensity during the pushdowns will not be reduced. Although your body becomes trained to recover faster at the end of a set of repetitions, overall fatigue may be experienced when initiating such a training system. When this occurs, your training intensity during the second exercise may be (initially) lower than expected. But through such a training process, your body becomes more capable of maintaining a higher level of intensity.

Another training system, called *trisetting,* is similar to supersetting, only you perform three sets of repetitions of either the same exercise, with a weight reduction for each consecutive set; three different exercises for the same muscle group; or an exercise for three separate muscle groups.

As with supersetting, the triset system of training increases your training volume. Similarly, weights have to be reduced with each consecutive set of repetitions. Your repetition goals will determine how much you need to reduce the resistance. But as you condition your body for such training, the reductions in resistance will likely be less.

To perform three different exercises for the same muscle group, you can increase your intensity of training simply through variety. For your triceps you may elect to perform lying French curls first, followed by dumbbell French curls, then pushdowns. Just keep in mind that by the time you reach the latter two exercises, your triceps already should be prefatigued and you will be required to use lighter-than-normal weights.

By following the triset system for three separate muscle groups, you certainly can save time in your training. However, it's difficult to maintain a high intensity of training when beginning such a system. You may decide to perform a set of repetitions in the bench press, followed by bicep curls, then by calf raises. Remember not to follow your first exercise with other exercise movements that are assisted by the first muscle group. For instance, it's unproductive to do bicep curls before seated rows because your biceps assist in the rowing motion and will subsequently fatigue during rows before your latissimus dorsi muscles will fatigue.

A third system is *circuit training,* geared toward improving your aerobic condition—your heart and lung systems. You simply perform a set of repetitions of one exercise, then immediately proceed to another exercise for a different muscle group. This nonstop procedure is followed until your total body is trained. Although circuit training is best performed on machines, since they are easily preset for resistance and ready to use, it is possible to train with dumbbells and barbells. But, the exercise devices must be prepared before the actual workout begins.

The most important consideration of circuit training, other than training intensity, is the rest time between exercises. We recommend you allow 30sec between exercises at first, then gradually reduce this rest period to 15sec. Through body adaptations to such exercise, you will become more capable of reducing this rest time without sacrificing your training intensity during the exercises. As you will see, circuit training elevates your heart rate and breathing—two parameters required for aerobic exercise.

Pre-exhaustion is another way of saving time during your workouts without lowering your training volume. You do this by exercising a muscle in its primary motion using an exercise that isolates a particular muscle, then follow with an exercise that uses the muscle in an assisting movement. An example is the combination of dumbbell flyes for your chest, supersetted with a set of bench presses. If you know your anatomy and physiology, you'll realize that your chest muscles are isolated during the flyes, and assist your anterior deltoids and triceps in the movement of raising a bar during the bench press. This is a means of increasing your training intensity.

The *forced repetitions* method is another alternative. When you are unable to perform another strict repetition in any exercise, your partner can help you lift a weight, but only as much as necessary to maintain slow movement. This forces your muscles to work at their then-maximal abilities. Remember, you first fatigue your muscles during the initially required number of repetitions, and while still able to lower the weight under your own control, have help (by another) in raising the weight.

This high-intensity system of training should be used sparingly, and is not recommended to use within four days prior to a race due to the increased time requirement for complete recovery.

Negative repetitions (don't let the name fool you; these repetitions are very productive in training for strength) refers to an eccentric contraction—the forceful lengthening of a muscle when it is under tension. Since your eccentric muscle strength is roughly 40 percent greater than your concentric strength (raising a weight), you will be required to prefatigue your muscles either by way of a strict set of repetitions first, or by increasing the weight load before performing any negatives.

Unbeknown to most strength enthusiasts, there are two categories of negative repetitions: *negatives* and *true negatives*. A negative refers to your own controlled lowering of a weight while the respective muscles are under tension. A true negative refers to a more forceful lengthening of a muscle when it's under tension—done by attempting to stop the movement at all points during the lowering phase of a repetition. This forces your muscles to lengthen under tremendous tension.

Since negative repetitions place such demand on your muscles and subsequently require additional recovery time along with producing the greatest amount of muscle soreness, we do not recommend negatives of any sort during your racing season.

Holistic training is a combination of various types of training formats (such as repetition ranges) to which your body adapts in differing ways—various energy systems and muscle fibers (slow- vs. fast-twitch) are stressed. In essence, this training maximizes development of the total muscle cell.

Holistic training can be done easily with use of dumbbells. Let's take the bicep curl, for instance. You can train holistically by performing a set of eight to twelve power-repetitions with say, 45lb dumbbells, immediately pick up a pair of 25lb dumbbells (for about fifteen slow reps), and immediately do another set of eight to twelve power-repetitions with 35lb dumbbells. Then, without stopping, use a pair of 15lb dumbbells for another fifteen to twenty slow repetitions. As you can see, you are stressing both your fast-twitch and slow-twitch fibers. If you try this system of training, you will notice the need for a high-intensity level of training.

Another option is to use the *power training* method. When you are concerned with the development of power and the subsequent increase in speed, you should incorporate explosive and accelerated movements when raising resistance during an exercise. Explosive repetitions improve your ability to activate a high number of muscle cells at one time, which means more powerful and faster movements. This helps your legs respond more quickly while running or changing direction of movement, like when the pit crew must reach a race vehicle during a pit stop. Accelerated repetitions train your muscles to maintain a high recruitment of muscle fibers, thus producing more power (and speed) during movements like running.

In essence, both explosion and acceleration increase your muscular force output, which translates to speed. An example is when you do calf raises. Since your calf muscles produce much of the propelling movements during any type of running, such power training will, without doubt, make you faster on your feet. You do this by first performing a set of, say, fifteen repetitions of standing calf raises, in a slow, rhythmic manner. Then when you reach muscular fatigue, lower your heels downward slowly and respond by rising up on the balls of your feet, as fast as possible. Remember, you must explode during the initial ascent upward, then maintain this muscle stimulation by accelerating throughout the remainder of the movement. This system increases your training intensity and requires additional time for complete recovery.

Plyometric training is another valuable means to improve your power and speed. This type of training is explained in detail later in the chapter.

The last alternative, *integrated training*, allows you to combine different training formats into your total training program. For instance, you can perform power-speed training together with strength training. Or you can combine training formats for muscle hypertrophy (enlargement) of fast-twitch muscle fibers with that designed for slow-twitch fiber enlargement. This can easily be accomplished in two separate ways.

75

First, while exercising each muscle group twice a week, each training format can be followed on separate days. That is, one day can be designed for one format while the following workout for the same muscle groups is designed for another format.

Your second option is to combine the two training formats into a single regimen. For this option we recommend performing your large muscle group exercises (multi-joint movements) like the bench press, squat or leg press, seated press, and so on, by way of heavier weight, higher intensity training, and performing the smaller, more isolated muscle group exercises in a lighter resistance type of training. For example, the exercises that stress those muscle groups used in specific motorsports movements should be trained using a power-speed method. The sample workout programs in chapter 8 may better illustrate this point.

As already discussed, each training format has its own repetition range and recommended rest period, with differing effects from each type of training. By following a well-structured program of integrated training, recovery from intense training (usually heavy weights and a low number of repetitions) is enhanced during the lighter, higher repetition training.

These systems of training can add variety to your workouts, but more importantly, each contributes in its own way to specific results. Be smart about the way you use the systems. Remember, those methods that require additional recovery time should not be used just prior to a race.

5.17 When You're on the Road

When you are traveling, whether for racing or for other reasons, usually the last thing you have time for is exercise. Being away from home for a week or so can be long enough to lose some of the benefits achieved from your exercise program. Therefore, it is important to spend at least a *little* time stimulating your body to maintain those benefits you've worked so hard to achieve.

You can travel with a pair or two of dumbbells or pack away surgical tubing. Surgical tubing is often made of an elastic latex material that offers resistance as it is stretched. It can be cut any length to adapt to almost any exercise. However, this may be more bother than it is worth because you have other, more practical alternatives.

Calisthenics and stretching should suffice. When performed correctly, these movements will maintain your strength and flexibility and perhaps improve them. In addition, such exercise may help to improve blood flow to your tissues. But this is providing they are done properly. What you'll find in photo sequences throughout this chapter is a series of recommended calisthenics and stretches that can be performed in any hotel room, in less

than 30min. As you will see, these calisthenics are not done in a traditional manner. Rather, they have been modified to increase productivity. That is, they will do more for you.

To make the exercises more functional, we have recommended that you add objects (of significant weight) to a duffel bag or a rolled-up towel, to increase resistance. Ideally, you should be capable of performing as few as ten repetitions, but not more than forty repetitions in each exercise before reaching momentary muscular failure.

Keep in mind that every stretch should be held for nearly 10sec in order to allow the muscles, tendons, and connective tissues time to relax and stretch. If when in a stretched position the respective muscles do not relax, let up a little because you have taken the stretch too far.

5.18 Recovering from Injury

When you do become injured, there are certain measures you can take to improve your recovery. To start out, it is advised that when you first notice pain (not to be confused with muscle soreness), you should be checked by your doctor. Now this doesn't mean every little ache and pain; it means an annoying injury that inhibits full movement or function of any part of your body.

Don't ignore the injury. It's a fool who relies on it to get better by itself. Ignoring an injury is a problem that often results in more serious damage, causing impaired performance and possibly a layoff from racing.

Although each injury has a specific path to follow before full function is returned, there are some procedures that can help speed the recovery process as opposed to letting the injury heal itself.

While pain resulting from an injury is present, rest is the key to recovery. Pain is a signal that lets you know your body is hurt. Any efforts made to overpower this signal are likely to make the injury worse.

Once pain is reduced significantly, you should begin a gradual stretching program for the muscles, tendons, ligaments, and connective tissues that are affected by the injury.

Note: Tight muscles can cause pain and prolong your recovery from injury. So keep your muscles strong *and* flexible.

Stretching will also aid recovery by increasing blood flow to the moving muscles and nearby tissues. However, at no point during stretching should you experience pain. If you do, discontinue carrying the movement to that point. The key is to stop the movement just shy of the point of pain. Gradually, you will be able to go further and further in the movement.

When full range of motion is attained, you should gradually return to resistance training. If you look at the tables in the book, you'll see that your initial resistance training rehabilitation begins with the use of light weights and high repetitions (fifteen to forty repetitions per set), at an effort level (Rating of Perceived Exertion) that is "very easy." It is likely that a limited range of motion will be used at first, but a gradual increase should start to occur within one to two weeks. However, you should never carry any exercise to the point of pain within the exercise movement. Perform one set of each exercise recommended for rehabilitation of the injured body part until a complete range of motion in all rehabilitation exercises is possible.

The resistance training significantly improves blood flow to the injured area, while maintaining or enhancing nerve-muscle functions. The longer the disuse of a body part, the more nerve-muscle function is lost. In the event of lengthy immobilization of say at least two weeks, a reeducation of nerve and muscle interaction may need to take place.

Once a complete range of motion is possible during initial resistance training rehabilitation, you can gradually increase your training volume or rather the number of sets you are performing. Perhaps you might increase to two sets of each rehabilitation exercise for week two, then three sets for week three.

Providing no pain is felt during any of these three rehabilitation sets, you should begin to gradually increase your training intensity. You do this by increasing the weights or any other form of resistance you are using, decreasing the repetitions you are performing, and simply working a little harder—a *little* harder, not *a lot*. Since your initial resistance training rehabilitation recommends that you perform between fifteen and forty repetitions per set, your next step is to lower your repetition range to twelve to fifteen reps.

To maintain a reasonable training effort, this means adding approximately 5-10 percent more weight in most exercises. Make sure the poundages you are using are of a gradual increase. This can mean adding 5 percent today, but if this is still too easy for you, add another 5 percent next workout. Don't add more than 10 percent for any one workout during rehabilitation, though.

A mistake that is often made by doctors and physical therapists is the recommendation to stop all resistance training when injured. First, we believe that most doctors should not offer advice about exercise or nutrition, for that matter. Unless a doctor is educated in sports medicine or exercise and nutrition, their knowledge about these matters can be severely limited—or almost nonexistent. Even some "physical therapists" are dangerously misinformed. Our suggestion to you: Search out a qualified sports medicine doctor.

To stop all resistance training during injury is simply bad advice. Not only does strength training of uninjured body parts help to maintain some nerve-muscle function in the injured body part, it also helps to increase blood flow to the injured part. In addition, training other muscles helps to limit the atrophy of the injured body part, which occurs as a result of disuse. Atrophy is defined as a loss of size, tissue, and function of various tissues as a result of disuse. Of course some modifications may need to be made in your training regimen, but the importance of continuing training is unquestionable.

It is also important that you follow smart eating habits by eating five times a day. Your protein consumption should be increased slightly to promote repair and recovery of injured tissues. But make sure your protein is of high quality—egg whites, meat, low-fat or no-fat dairy products, fish, poultry, or even 100 percent egg white protein powder. A multiple vitamin or mineral supplement is also recommended to ensure adequate intake of these important nutrients.

With the help of our scientific community, we have found various therapeutic modalities that enhance recovery from injury. For instance, the application of ice and heat (at separate times) can limit swelling accompanying tissue damage (cold), and increase blood flow to the injured muscles (cold and heat). These techniques aid in the removal of waste products (such as carbon dioxide) while delivering nutrient-rich blood to the muscles for repair.

Whirlpool treatments work in a manner similar to that of heat applications, with an added benefit of improved relaxation. Relaxation is also a benefit of massage. Through massage, the manipulation of the tissues causes increased blood flow to and from the muscles. You should already know why this helps in the recovery process.

It should also be of no surprise to you that your muscles recover while you are sleeping. If your sleep is interrupted, and you don't feel rested, chances are your injured tissues are not healing as fast as they should. Remember, it's not only physically stressful situations like strength training that place more demands on you for additional amounts of sleep; injury places these same increased demands on your body for recovery.

Much of the same goes for daily amounts of stress. Since stress places additional demands on you, both physically and mentally, high levels of stress can lead to prolonged recovery times.

Stretching can aid in improving recovery from injury. As a matter of fact, it is a technique used before any resistance training is begun during rehabilitation. Proper stretching can relax muscle tension often accompanying injury. It also increases blood flow to injured tissues. But you must be careful when stretching following injury—you can overdo it. Go by "feel." That is, take each stretch to the point of where the muscle tissue either gradually "relaxes" while the stretch is being held, or just shy of any point of pain. By forcing your muscles and tendons to stretch under too much stress, you can cause additional microtrauma to the tissues. This alone can place additional demands on your body for recovery.

Electrical muscle stimulation (EMS) is another technique used to improve recovery following injury. EMS is especially useful when immobilization of a body part is required. When small loads of intermittent electrical current are sent through skin-applied electrodes, large nerves are stimulated to in turn stimulate muscle contraction. The continual process of contraction (electric current), relaxation (no current), contraction, and so on, allows for greater blood flow to the area. In addition, proper use of EMS reduces muscle spasms often experienced after injury, and permits a muscle to remain more relaxed. This relaxation also permits blood to flow more easily.

Perhaps the most recent technique that shows promise for improving recovery from injury as well as exercise is laser treatment. Low-level lasers stimulate nerves by permitting changes in tissues at even the smallest (ultrastructure) levels. It is done in the absence of heat . Although quite complicated, energy that is taken from light is transmitted to the injured tissues at very low levels— less than one watt. Low-level laser treatment tends to be effective with conditions like tendinitis, bursitis, wound healing, and connective tissue repair. Presently, the US Food and Drug Administration (FDA) rules the use of low-level lasers as a nonsignificant risk, but it is currently studying its effectiveness.

5.19 Plyometric Training for the Crew

In order to reduce time spent in the pits (when applicable), crew members must be able to get to the vehicle to perform duties in a timely fashion and to get away from the vehicle when duties are completed—all as quickly as possible. That means these individuals must be fast on their feet and able to exert above-normal forces with each step. Plyometrics can help them do just that.

Plyometrics is simply the display of explosiveness after intense overloading of the muscles, resulting in greater speed and power. In essence, such training increases your ability to recruit additional numbers of muscle cells to become activated at one time; in simpler terms, it enables you to use more muscle during a particular movement, like running and stopping and running again.

This may be better explained by describing a scenario of muscle contraction. Let's say that an untrained individual can voluntarily contract 30 percent of the muscle cells of a given muscle. Through strength training alone, this individual becomes capable of recruiting 50 percent of the available muscle cells. Through the practice of strength training and plyometrics, this same individual becomes able to contract 65 percent of the muscle cells. Now which training technique do you think produces greater force output? Anyone shy of being an outright fool will undoubtedly select the 65 percent recruitment technique. This practice makes you move faster, and can be learned through proper training.

To understand the basic physiology of plyometrics, you first must know the three types of muscle contraction. They are:

1. Concentric contraction: The shortening of a muscle under tension. It's what happens when you raise a weight upward. An example is the raising of a dumbbell during an arm curl.

2. Isometric, or static, contraction: When a muscle contracts without any movement. This is done by placing force against an immovable object.

3. Eccentric contraction: When a muscle is lengthened under tension, like during the lowering (of the weight) phase of an exercise. Your muscles are at least 40 percent stronger in this type of contraction as compared to a concentric contraction. Eccentric contractions contribute greatly to strength, speed, and power development.

With plyometrics and speedy performance, the most important considerations are the eccentric contractions and the transition to concentric contractions. The quicker you cushion your body when hitting the ground (eccentric contraction) and respond by pushing off the ground (concentric contraction), the faster you get to and from the racing vehicle.

The idea behind plyometric training is to facilitate maximal eccentric contraction which develops maximal muscle tension; then to switch to a concentric contraction for your desired movement. All of this is done in milliseconds.

When performing plyometrics, your goal is to get maximal explosive force in the shortest amount of time. Through proper performance, benefits in power and speed can be experienced as early as four to five plyometric training sessions.

You'll see in this chapter two valuable samples of plyometric training that are ideal for increasing the ability of the pit crew to get to and from a race car in record time. Keep in mind that the main concept of plyometric training is to practice "exploding," and think about spending as little time on the ground and as much time in the air as possible. Although several other plyometric movements can be helpful, we feel that these two techniques will be most helpful and won't take much time away from your busy racing schedule.

Strength is a prerequisite for plyometric training. If your muscles and tendons are not already strong, plyometrics can cause injury. Because plyometric movements are stressful on your tissues, your tissues must be capable of handling such high levels of force.

Four weeks of strength training is a minimum recommendation before beginning plyometric training. Failure to do so can result in injuries such as strains and tendinitis. To make sure you are adequately warmed up, perform your plyometric training about ten to fifteen minutes after your strength training workouts.

5.20 Understanding Muscle Soreness

Some scientists say muscles become sore from damage incurred during exercise like that of strength training. Others claim the damage and soreness is a result of minute connective tissue tears. State-of-the-art information indicates that both contentions are probably correct.

Muscle soreness caused by (muscle) cell damage resulting from exercise differs from that resulting from a strain or a tear. You should know that the pain associated with muscle soreness usually diminishes within a few days after intense exercise. Of course if it doesn't, you will want to consult your doctor. Should a strain or tear occur, you will need to see your doctor *right away*. When exercise produces sore muscles, a doctor is not needed, but sensible training and dietary practices are.

Muscle tissue damage and delayed muscle soreness (occurring a day or two following exercise) have been monitored through the measurements of myoglobin (oxygen-storing elements within the muscles) and muscle enzymes found in the blood. By discovering substances most often found inside muscle cells present in the blood, it is believed that damage occurs to some of the cellular components. In some cases, this damage allows proteins to escape into extracellular spaces (outside muscle cells).

Researchers have also found evidence of muscle damage following exercise through the detection of muscle cell breakdown and the accumulation of phagocytes (cells that destroy harmful cells) and erythrocytes (hemoglobin-containing substances in your blood that transport oxygen) within the muscle cells themselves.

It appears that minute tears within the connective tissue around the muscle may be produced during exercise. Abraham's work (*Medicine and Science in Sports and Exercise*, 1977) describes the rationale for this contention. This researcher discovered a rise in hydroxyproline (a naturally occurring amino acid) in the urine of those performing bench-stepping exercise. Since this amino acid is found primarily in the connective tissue, it is believed that tension or force production associated

with muscular contractions might damage connective tissue as well.

It is evident that strength training frequently produces muscle damage and soreness. Therefore, precautions must be taken to ensure muscle repair and growth. No doubt you have heard that muscles need to be broken down before they can rebuild and adapt to their stimulus (training). This is true, to an extent. Therefore, you must cycle your training. Cycle training will help to provide a more complete approach to muscle recovery following exercise. Because constant heavy training can cause continuous damage to muscle tissues, adequate low-to-moderate intensity work, together with sufficient rest and smart eating, should become important parts of any exercise regimen.

You should vary your poundages, repetition ranges, and rest time between sets and exercises to ensure holistic training and subsequent recovery. You'll find no improvement, and many times a reduction in performance, if you stick with any strength training program for more than eight to twelve weeks. Cycling your training is very important for this reason.

For many years, muscle soreness and damage have been linked with eccentric muscle contractions. Remember, eccentric contractions are characterized by a forceful lengthening of the muscle when it is under tension. When muscular work, especially that involving eccentric contractions, is performed without adequate recuperation between exercise bouts, your muscle force output lowers significantly. In addition, strength is reduced for longer periods when eccentric contractions are performed. For this reason alone, racing personnel should not perform any eccentric or negative-only repetitions during the competitive racing season.

Other techniques that are helpful in reducing muscle soreness include the application of ice on strenuously worked muscles following exercise. This can help to reduce swelling and pain that often occur after intense strength training.

Although somewhat controversial at the present time, it is believed that stretching can help reduce muscle soreness. Those who advocate stretching after workouts contend that stretching relaxes the muscles, permitting a quicker recovery and less chance of soreness. Others believe the damage is already done and stretching will not contribute to any reduction in muscle soreness.

As you may well realize, any technique that promotes recovery may help to reduce muscle soreness. Another technique for reducing muscle soreness is the application of heat, in the form of hot showers, sauna, or whirlpool. Since heat promotes blood flow to selected areas, such a technique may play a part in reducing soreness following intense exercise. But the best benefits are obtained when these heat treatments are used immediately after exercise.

Chapter 6

Getting Started and Continuing

*If success in racing is paramount in your life, you must ensure that the
incentive to exercise is as strong as your will to win.
Properly directing the forces that motivate you is a form of success.*

If racing greatness is paramount in your life, it becomes your duty to ensure that the incentive to exercise is as strong as your will to win. By properly directing the forces that motivate you, you *will* achieve your goals.

6.1 Motivation

Since you're likely involved in some type of motorsports activity, we can assume that you have a will to win. And since you have been prompted to read this book, it can also be assumed that you also have a will to succeed. In essence, you have an unquestionable interest in making yourself a better driver.

Although you are highly motivated to excel on the racetrack, in the pits, in the garage, or simply on the highway, a similar motivation to exercise is sometimes difficult to come by. We all can come up with an infinite number of excuses why not to exercise. But most often, they are just that—excuses. Surely we can find time to train if we really want to, even with a hectic schedule like that of a professional racer.

To be the best you can be is a motivating force in strength training. Initially, your aggressive desire to succeed in motorsports is what motivates you to begin a strength training program.

A primary factor affecting motivation is goal-setting. It's clear that you are goal-oriented—you have to be, or there would be no place for you in the world of motorsports. No doubt, your interest in strength training to improve your abilities is based on goal-orientation—with the goal to be the best. Goal-setting is also a prerequisite for exercise

success. And along with your long-range goals of becoming a better driver or crew member, you must also set short-range goals to help you continue with and succeed in your strength training.

Short-range goals must be set realistically, within your current competence level. That is, you cannot expect to become Mr. America or another Mark Martin overnight. Small measures of improvement eventually add up to greater successes.

There are several ways to help motivate yourself to improve your physical and mental capabilities. Incentives play a large part in your participation in the iron game. Just the idea of looking and feeling better is motivation enough for many people. For those whose livelihood revolves around racing, financial rewards may be a primary motivation.

So, it is crucial that you become motivated about your exercise program. We all know that pain and frustration sometimes lead to resentment and avoidance of exercise. But this happens only when exercise is not begun at an appropriate pace, that is, slowly and gradually. By beginning your strength training program at a low to moderate intensity, coupled with a small volume of work, you are less likely to experience annoying and sometimes unproductive muscle soreness.

Once you get yourself into a workout regimen and begin to "feel" some results, you will become more inclined to stay motivated and to keep "pumpin' up." When you actually start to see the results via your physical appearance, you'll be more highly motivated to continue.

You learn to convert negative feedback into positive motivation. For instance, pain is a negative sensory perception that can be used in a positive manner. Obviously, no one likes pain. But when you know it's doing some good, your attitude about it may change. As you gradually increase your training intensity, you will likely feel some additional pain from muscle soreness. Then you know that you are again working hard enough to receive additional benefits. Just keep in mind that you need not always be sore in order to benefit from your training.

Much the same goes for that "training fatigue" you'll experience at the end of a workout. You know that your workout session has been beneficial.

As you train for longer periods, you will begin to realize which motivating forces work for you. Some people are motivated to look better, some want to feel better, while others want to perform better. Everyone is different. Regardless of the motivating force behind the drive to exercise, reminding yourself of why you are exercising will make you strive to continue.

Try to avoid interruptions during your workout time. Constant interruptions distract you, interrupt your concentration, and reduce your ability to remain motivated.

Once you have experienced that awesome "pumped up" feeling, you'll know how good it feels. But remember, you won't always feel that pump—and you don't need to in order to benefit from your strength training. As your training progresses, the pumped-up feeling serves as a signal that you have reached your goals. It allows you to feel some temporary "beneficial effects" from the exercise.

You can and should challenge your own capabilities by continually striving to use heavier weights or performing additional repetitions in any given exercise. This shows objective improvement. Without improvement, you'll never be motivated to continue your exercise.

By becoming aggressive in your training, just as you are in your racing or driving, you will consequently increase your ability to keep your motivation high. You can actually learn to "psyche yourself" to literally assault the weights, believing that the sky's the limit in how much you can lift. But please keep in mind that your form in exercise is still the most important consideration.

Being receptive to assistance can be another motivator. Such assistance, as long as it's from qualified personnel, can add variety to your workouts so they remain interesting. The same applies to cycling your training. By simply switching to another format of training, you are less likely to remain stable or plateau in your performance. Failure to improve can lead to boredom and a subsequent layoff from training.

It may be easier for you to keep others highly motivated to exercise, than it is to keep yourself motivated. As a training partner, friend, or colleague, your compliments go a long way. And since we all like compliments, this reinforcement can add to anyone's motivation to exercise.

On the other hand, it make take a crude comment to stimulate you to begin working out. Just think how it feels to hear someone tell you that you're looking quite plump, or ask you why your clothes no longer fit you. These are negative comments that can be turned into positive motivators, providing you handle them in a mature fashion and act on them. Knowing that an unfit individual cannot perform as well as one who is in good shape, hopefully you'll begin to question your own performance. When this happens, you know it's time to exercise.

A business manager or race team owner can surely benefit (financially) by taking a few seconds to let a driver or pit crew member know that his or her efforts are well recognized. This can be the biggest motivator of all.

6.2 Minimum Recommendations for Exercise

There are minimum recommendations for obtaining strength training benefits. You can exercise each major muscle group as little as twice a week and still improve your strength. However, your training efforts must be nothing short of intense. This means every set of repetitions (excluding warm-ups) should be carried to the point of momentary muscular failure—and beyond (such as through forced repetitions and negatives). Although one work set of each exercise may suffice, two or three are better for results. Of course, this will depend on how much time you have allotted yourself for exercise. It is also important that you go no more than 96hr between any two workouts.

But if you can allow three days or more to devote to your exercise, benefits will be experienced sooner and to a greater degree. That is, you'll get into better shape faster.

For best results, and as a time-saver, each work set of repetitions must be taken to the point of muscular failure. With this quality of training in mind while you are undertaking a circuit-training program, you must maintain this intensity for a minimum of 20-30min in order to improve your cardiovascular system.

Generally speaking, when following a three-day-a-week strength training program, allow 48-96hr of rest between workouts of a particular muscle group—no more and no less.

Aerobic conditioning can be beneficial when you perform appropriate endurance-type exercise for at least 20min twice a week. However, three times a week, for a similar length of time, works better. Regardless of the exercise you are participating in (walking, cycling, cross-country skiing), you should find yourself somewhere between sweatlessness and discomfort.

To be more scientific, you can calculate the work level of your heart rate by way of your radial pulse, which is located near your thumb, on the underside of your wrist. By counting the number of (heart) beats for a 6sec period and multiplying by ten, you can determine your heart rate per minute. This should fall within a recommended training zone of 60-85 percent of your age-predicted maximal heart rate. The rate can be found by subtracting your age from 220, then multiplying the percentages (0.60 and 0.85) by this number. The minimum recommendations for achieving beneficial cardiovascular effects is 60 percent. Of course, the better aerobic condition you are in, the harder you'll need to exercise to raise your heart rate to a desired level.

6.3 Maximum Recommendations for Exercise

It is unlikely that you, as a racing enthusiast with limited time for exercise, will need to be concerned with spending too much time in the gym. But we feel you should know what the limits are in exercising.

The major problem that occurs with excessive exercise is overtraining. As described in Chapter 5, overtraining is basically a time when your body decides to take its own break from being overworked. In most cases, it is caused by a lack of recovery from exercise and it often leads to a reduction in physical and mental performance. This is when you do too much, too soon.

You definitely are overtraining if you don't allow at least 48hr of rest between workouts of your skeletal muscles, with the possible exceptions of your neck, abdominal, and perhaps your calf exercises. The more intensely you train, together with the higher your training volume (numbers of exercises and sets), the longer you need to facilitate complete recovery.

Looking at the recovery time table, you can determine the longest length of time needed for recovery. By taking longer rest periods between workouts of a given muscle group, benefits achieved can soon dwindle.

We do not recommend that any strength training session last for more than 90min because more of the muscle-building hormone, testosterone, is released during short, intense workouts of about 45-60min. Longer training periods tend to suppress the release of this hormone. A 90min workout lets you do what you need without significantly lowering peak testerone levels.

More and more research is showing that you receive increased benefits from doing less (than traditionally believed) but at higher levels of intensity.

Hours and hours of training often lead to mental and physical fatigue, which often leads to injury. If you cannot accomplish what you want in 60-90min, then you're somehow wasting time.

You must keep your perspective: You're not a bodybuilder, so there's no need to train like one. In fact, to be a smart bodybuilder, you would train two or three times a day for no more than 1hr each session.

When training aerobically, there's no need to do it more than four times a week for 30min a session. As long as your training is of sufficient quality (intense enough), you will get everything you need from it—in a cardiovascular sense. Similarly, you're not a marathon runner, so you need not train like one either. In fact, there's no need for maximal aerobic endurance in any type of motorsports performance.

6.4 Adapting to Time Allotments

Regularity is sometimes referred to as "the key to exercise success." If your objection is that you don't like to exercise or you simply do not have time for it, it really doesn't matter because the variety offered with strength training can be structured to meet your individual needs—and time allotments. So now what's your excuse?

With the numerous hours spent working on your racing vehicle, whether you do it part time or full time, you probably don't have that much time to dedicate to exercise, even though you may realize the importance of it.

There is one major rule to follow once you decide how much time you'll devote to strength training, and that is: Quality is more important than quantity! It is better to do fewer exercises, but do them correctly and intensely, than it is to spend hours that are virtually wasted, performing your exercises in a haphazard manner.

With the idea of doing fewer (exercises) but working harder, it is impossible not to find a reasonable amount of time to work out. Remember your goals. If you want to *be* the best, you need to *work* for it—it doesn't come naturally.

If you have access to machines like Nautilus, Pyramid (a great choice), Weider equipment, or even Universal-type equipment, you will spend less time preparing your workout stations. In fact, many machines have multiple workout stations that can be set by means of simply sliding a pin into a weight stack. Some machines require a simple seat adjustment. Whatever the adjustments, machines don't require much time to prepare for use.

Contrary to what many foolish muscleheads preach, you can accomplish the same goals with machines as you can with free weights. It's only musclehead ignorance that says you can't. You and those making such claims must take into consideration that you are not training to be a bodybuilder. Your goal is to exhibit superior motorsports performance.

You can structure your resistance-training program in any way you find necessary to accommodate your time availability. For instance, you can train selected body parts (the lower body, for example) on one day and others (the upper body) on the following day. This type of scheduling allows you to spend less time during each workout session while performing a larger volume of exercise per body part. But it requires you to train at least four times a week. More specific examples are illustrated in Chapter 8.

When you use free weights (barbells and dumbbells), you'll be required to take the time to place weights on the bars for your various exercises (obviously you won't be using the same weights for every exercise). If a complete line of dumbbells is available to you, you can save time by simply picking up an appropriate pair for a respective exercise. When barbells are your only source of resistance, rest time between sets and exercises can be spent preparing another bar for the following exercise.

As already stated, free weights, as barbells and dumbbells are commonly called, can produce the same results as machines. However, free weights require two additional parameters: balance and form. Machines often dictate your form and provide a balanced resistance, while barbells require your own assessment of balance and form. And although you can become injured with machine exercise, there is a slightly higher risk involved when using free weights.

But don't fret. If you follow proper procedures, as outlined in this book, chances of getting injured are remote.

When you complement your strength training with aerobic exercise, you are exercising in a holistic manner. That is, you are promoting the conditioning of all your major systems (heart, lungs, skeletal muscles, nerves, and so on). However, this can be done through circuit training, too. Chapter 8 gives some examples of how this can be accomplished.

When conditioning your cardiovascular system separately from your strength training program, there are certain considerations to keep in mind.

Although benefits begin to occur after about 5min of aerobic exercise, it takes roughly 20min for significant effects to take place. Whether you use a bike, a treadmill, a cross-country skiing simulator, a stepper, or a rower, similar cardiovascular benefits can be achieved, as long as you do it correctly.

Keeping in mind that quality is more important than quantity, you must train aerobically at a level of effort that places you somewhere between sweatlessness and discomfort. Training aerobically simply refers to an appropriate level of effort that is sustained for a period of time. Our recommended period is 20-30min. This includes a 5min warm-up at low intensity, along with a 5min cool-down.

When you get bored, and you can very quickly with most types of exercise, you need variety. Although most exercise physiologists recognize cross-country skiing as a superior form of aerobic exercise (since it utilizes a greater amount of muscle mass), you can add variety by exercising on say a cross-country skier for 10min, a rower for another 10min, and a bike for 10min.

Whatever your choice of equipment, you must quality train for three to four times a week to obtain the best results. More is not better. In fact, it would be more advantageous for you as a racer to dedicate any extra time you have (in excess of three 20-30min periods a week) to strength training.

Chapter 7

Illustrated Performance

*It's often said that a picture is worth a thousand words.
It's also said that practice makes habit. To develop proper exercise
customs is to take one giant step toward greatness.*

It's often said that a picture is worth a thousand words. It's also said that practice makes habit. To develop proper exercise customs is to take one giant step toward greatness.

7.1 Productive Stretching Techniques

The following pictures illustrate head-to-toe stretches for selected body parts. Remember to hold each stretch for roughly 10sec to allow the respective muscles and tendons time to loosen up. Each stretch that you select should be performed at least three times. Remember, for those stretches affecting only one side of your body, repeat the same procedure for the other side.

Chest stretch between benches. *Primary body part(s) affected: Chest. Anchor your upper body between two benches by placing your hands on the benches at lower chest level. Slowly lower your upper body downward until the muscles of your chest tighten.*

Shoulder to wall stretch. *Primary body part(s) affected: Front of shoulder. Standing at arm's length from a wall, with your side facing the wall, position your hand on the wall at shoulder level. Gradually turn away from the wall until the muscles of your shoulder and/or chest tighten.*

Chest stretch against wall. *Primary body part(s) affected: Chest. Standing about 2 or 3ft away from a wall, with hand positioned slightly above waist level, gradually turn away from wall until the muscles of your chest and/or shoulder tighten.*

Shoulder bench stretch. *Primary body part(s) affected: Front of shoulder, chest. Anchor your upper body between two benches by placing your hands on the benches at shoulder level. Slowly lower your upper body downward until the muscles of your shoulders tighten. To make sure your elbows are positioned perpendicular to your upper body, you may need to turn your hands so your thumbs are facing you.*

Neck, shoulder stretch. *Primary body part(s) affected: Neck, upper shoulders. Grasp both hands in front of your body, at chin level, with arms straight out. Reach forward as far as possible until the muscles of your neck and shoulders tighten. To stretch the neck muscles, gradually glide your chin backward. Warning: Do not tilt your head backward—only glide your chin.*

Spider walk up wall. *Primary body part(s) affected: Shoulders, middle back. Standing near and facing a wall, slowly walk up the wall (like a spider) by letting your fingers do the walking. "Walk" up the wall with the intention of touching the ceiling, and concentrate on the "reach" when your hand is as high as possible.*

Arm across chest stretch. *Primary body part(s) affected: Upper back, rear shoulder. Grasp your left arm above the elbow with your right hand, and gradually pull the left arm across your chest until your upper back and rear shoulder muscles tighten.*

Alternate knee to chest stretch. *Primary body part(s) affected: Lower, middle back. Position right arm around underside of your left knee and pull left knee toward right shoulder as you lift right shoulder up to meet left knee. Place left hand on floor near buttocks for balance.*

Knee to chest stretch. *Primary body part(s) affected: Lower back. Grasp one leg just below the knee cap and pull knee toward chest while lifting shoulders up and off floor. Force your lower back downward against floor.*

Sit-'n'-twist stretch. *Primary body part(s) affected: Lower, middle back. Seated on floor, place your right foot on the floor to the outside of your left knee. Position your right elbow against the inside of your right knee, and your left hand on the floor slightly behind and to the side of your left buttocks. Push against your right leg with your right elbow while you do the same with your left hand, attempting to turn your upper body to your left.*

Sit-'n'-reach stretch. *Primary body part(s) affected: Lower back. Seated on floor with legs slightly bent, grasp lower leg with hands and pull chest downward toward knees. Remember to "round-out" back.*

Hamstring stretch on floor. *Primary body part(s) affected: Rear upper leg. Sitting in an upright position on the floor, grasp the undersides of your knees with your hands. Arch your back as you pull your upper body downward toward your knees until the muscles of your rear, upper leg (hamstrings) tighten. Make sure to maintain an arched back throughout the movement.*

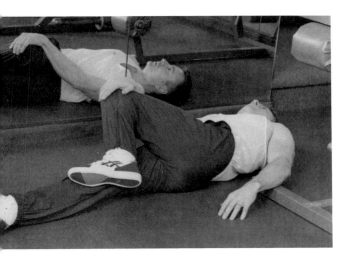

Buttock stretch. *Primary body part(s) affected: Buttocks, lower back. Lying flat on your back, place your left knee over your right leg as far as possible with your left foot off the floor. Grasp your left knee with your right hand and gently push it downward. You can place your left hand on the floor for balance.*

PNF sit-'n'-reach stretch (partner assisted). *Primary body part(s) affected: Lower back. While sitting on floor with knees slightly bent, allow partner to push your upper body downward toward knees until your lower back tightens. As your partner holds you in that position, gently (with only about 40 percent effort) attempt to push backward against your partner's resistance. Relax and allow your partner to push you downward again to the point where your lower back tightens. Then repeat.*

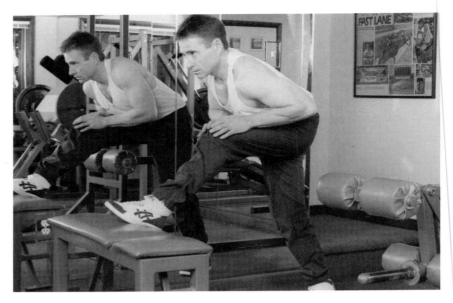

Two-leg calf stretch off step. *Primary body part(s) affected: Rear lower leg. Standing on a 2-4in block, with heels hanging off the block, lower your heels toward the floor as far as possible. To maintain balance, hold on to a stable object (such as a wall).*

Hamstring stretch on bench. *Primary body part(s) affected: Rear upper leg. Place your left foot on a bench, with leg bent and right foot positioned about 3 or 4ft behind you. Lean upper body forward and place hands on top of left knee. Gently straighten your left knee until your hamstring muscles tighten. You can provide a downward force against left knee with your hands, but remain leaning forward throughout the movement.*

Shin stretch. *Primary body part(s) affected: Front lower leg. With your heels anchored on a 2-4in block, gently lower your toes toward the floor until the muscles in the front of your lower legs tighten. To help balance yourself, hold on to a wall or another stable object.*

Hip flexor stretch. *Primary body part(s) affected: Front hip, thigh. Place your right leg, just below the knee, on a bench with your left foot anchored on floor about 2-3ft in front of the bench. Arch your back and push your right hip downward and forward to stretch your right hip flexor muscles.*

PNF thigh stretch. *Primary body part(s) affected: Thigh. Grasp your right ankle with your right hand and balance yourself by holding on to a stable object with your left hand. Lift your right foot upward with your hand while attempting to extend your right leg. Do not pull your ankle toward your buttocks. Attempt to maintain an 80-90 degree angle with the leg you are stretching.*

Spinal push-up stretch. *Primary body part(s) affected: Frontal, middle, lower spine. Lying face down on the floor, position your hands to your sides at lower stomach level and slowly extend your arms as your lower back arches. Caution: Push forward and upward to alleviate excessive back arch.*

One-leg calf stretch off step. *Primary body part(s) affected: Rear lower leg. Standing on a 2-4in block, with heels hanging off the block, gently shift your weight onto your left foot while lowering your left heel as far as possible toward the floor. Support your balance with your right foot while holding on to a wall or other stable object.*

7.2 Exercises Most Often Done Incorrectly

Now that you know what to do, you need to know how each exercise should be performed in order to get the most out of your workouts. Even the slightest improper movement or hand alignment can produce a less effective exercise and increase a risk of injury.

What follows is an illustration of how each of the forty-three exercises should be performed. This list constitutes only a small selection of exercises that can be performed for each muscle group.

Each exercise is shown in the extreme ranges of motion. Please note the proper hand and body positions. One rule to follow is that if you don't feel the muscles working (ones you are intending to work), something is wrong.

Remember also that each exercise should be performed in a slow, rhythmic manner unless otherwise suggested.

 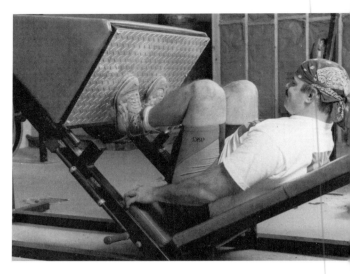

Exercise: Leg press (feet low). *Primary muscle(s) affected: Quadriceps (see squat exercise, above). Position your feet low on the standard of a leg press machine, with knees and toes in the same direction (first photo).*

Slowly lower the weight until your legs are slightly less than ninety degrees at the knee joint (second photo). Then push upward, but don't lock your knees. Keep the weight on the balls of your feet.

 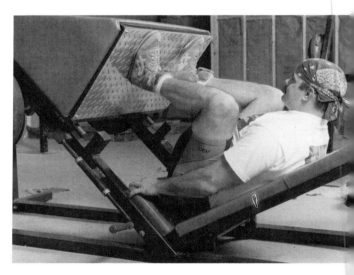

Exercise: Leg press (feet high). *Primary muscle(s) affected: Hamstrings (see squat exercise above). Position your feet high on the standard of a leg press machine, with toes slightly pointed outward (first photo). Slowly*

lower the weight until your knees are at a 90 degree angle (second photo). Then push upward, but don't lock your knees. Keep the weight on your heels.

Exercise: Squat. *Primary muscle(s) affected: Quadriceps, hamstrings (vastus lateralis, vastus medialis, vastus intermedius [not shown on chart] and the rectus femoris make up the quadriceps group) (biceps femoris and semitendinosus constitute the major muscles of the hamstrings). Take a bar off two supports (using a power rack, for instance) with a wider than shoulder width grip and bar resting on a comfortable spot on your upper shoulders. Feet should be positioned slightly more than shoulder width apart with toes angled slightly outward (first photo). Slowly lower your body until your upper legs are nearly parallel with the floor (second photo). Then rise upward to complete leg extension. Attempt to keep your back arched and weight on your heels throughout the movement.*

Exercise: Leg extensions. *Primary muscle(s) affected: Quadriceps (see squat exercise above). Sit with your knees just over the edge of a leg extension machine (first* photo). *Slowly extend your legs until your knees are almost straight (second photo). Pause, lower, and repeat.*

Exercise: Leg curl. *Primary muscle(s) affected: Hamstrings (see squat exercise above). Lie face down on a leg curl machine with your knees just over the edge of the bench (first photo). Slowly curl your leg upward, as far as possible, attempting to touch your heels to your buttocks (second photo). Pause, lower, and repeat. Try to keep your hips down on the pad.*

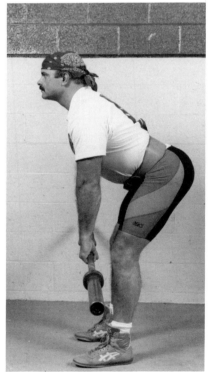

Exercise: Stiff-leg deadlift with an arched back (standing). *Primary muscle(s) affected: Hamstrings (see squat exercise above). Grasp a bar in front of your body, with arms extended and with a shoulder width grip and legs almost straight (first photo). Slowly lower the bar as far as possible, but keep your back arched (second photo). Pause, rise upward, and repeat.*

Exercise: Stiff-leg deadlift with an arched back (seated). *Primary muscle(s) affected: Hamstrings (see squat exercise above). Sitting with heels against the foot standards and legs nearly straight, grasp a bar connected to a cable around a low pulley in front of your body* *with extended arms, and position yourself on your back (first photo). With an arched back, slowly rise upward and forward until your hamstring muscles tighten (second photo). Pause, recline backward, and repeat.*

Exercise: Bench press. *Primary muscle(s) affected: Pectorals (pectoralis major). Grasp a bar from the standards of a bench press with a grip that's more than shoulder width, lift off, and position the bar directly above your chin (first photo). Slowly lower the bar until it comes in* *contact with your chest, at a point low on your chest (second photo). Pause, then push upward by directing the bar up and toward your head until your arms are locked, directly above your chin. Repeat.*

Exercise: Dumbbell bench press. Primary muscle(s) affected: Pectorals (see bench press exercise). Lie on your back with a dumbbell in each hand positioned at lower chest level (first photo). Push upward and toward your head until your arms are nearly extended (second photo). Make sure to position dumbbells directly over your chin when your arms are extended. Lower and repeat.

Exercise: Flye. Primary muscle(s) affected: Pectorals (see bench press exercise). Lie on your back with dumbbells at lower chest level, with thumbs up and arms nearly straight (first photo). Keeping your arms in a constant near-straightened position, raise the weights upward above your body while you gradually rotate the dumbbells so your little fingers approach each other and dumbbells almost touch (second photo). Pause, lower, and repeat. This movement is similar to "hugging a tree."

Exercise: Pec deck. *Primary muscle(s) affected: Pectorals (see bench press exercise). Position yourself on a pec deck machine with arms as far back as possible and elbows slightly lower than shoulder level (first photo). Pull your elbows toward each other using your forearms*

until elbows are in front of your body (second photo). Pause, return to a stretched position, and repeat. For best results, turn in your palms toward your face and concentrate on your chest muscles virtually pulling your elbows inward.

Exercise: Crossover. *Primary muscle(s) affected: Pectorals (see bench press exercise). Grasp the handles of a crossover machine with palms facing each other, feet in a stable position, elbows bent slightly, and arms out away from your body (first photo). Slowly pull elbows together*

until your hands approach each other (second photo). For best results, position your elbows toward the floor and keep slightly bent throughout the entire movement. Slowly return to starting position and repeat.

Exercise: Chest dip. *Primary muscle(s) affected: Pectorals (see bench press exercise). Positioned on dip bars, lower your upper body downward as far as possible—until your chest and/or shoulder muscles tighten (first photo). Lean forward and push your body upward until your shoulders are 4-5in higher than your elbows (second photo). Pause, lower, and repeat. Concentrate on using your chest muscles to pull your elbows downward.*

Exercise: Overhead press. *Primary muscle(s) affected: Anterior deltoid. Grasp a bar with a grip similar to that used during bench pressing, and lift bar off the stan-* *dards at near arms' length (first photo). Slowly lower the bar until it touches the top portion of your chest (second photo). Pause, raise the weight, and repeat.*

Exercise: Front deltoid raise. *Primary muscle(s) affected: Anterior deltoid. Holding on to a dumbbell, with thumb up, extend your slightly bent arm downward without allowing dumbbell to touch your thigh (first photo). Slowly raise dumbbell upward across your body until thumb is in front of your opposite eye (second photo). Pause, lower, and repeat.*

Exercise: Lateral raise. *Primary muscle(s) affected: Lateral deltoid (sometimes referred to as the medial deltoid). Grasp a dumbbell in each hand and position in front of each thigh with slightly bent arms (first photo). Slowly raise your elbows until they are level with your ears (second photo). Caution: Do not allow wrists to rise higher than your elbows at any time during the movement. Lower fully and repeat.*

Exercise: Upright row. *Primary muscle(s) affected: Lateral deltoid, posterior deltoid. Grasp a bar in front of your body, with arms fully extended and with a shoulder width grip (first photo). Leading with your elbows, slow-* *ly pull the bar upward until it touches your chin (second photo). Never allow your wrists to rise higher than your elbows. Lower and repeat.*

 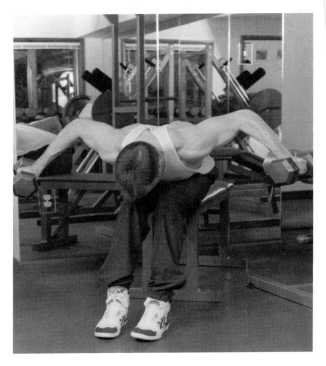

Exercise: Bent-over lateral raise. *Primary muscle(s) affected: Posterior deltoid. Sitting on a bench, with a dumbbell in each hand and slightly bent arms, while leaning forward with chest against knees, position* *dumbbells near your ankles (first photo). Slowly raise your elbows upward as far as possible, pause, lower, and repeat (second photo). Always make sure your elbows are higher than your wrists.*

Exercise: Shoulder shrug. *Primary muscle(s) affected: Trapezius. Grasp a bar with a close grip in front of your body with arms fully extended (first photo). Slowly shrug your shoulders upward as far as possible, as though you* *were attempting to touch your shoulders to your ears (second photo). Pause, lower, and repeat. Keep your arms straightened throughout the movement.*

Exercise: Reverse grip pulldown. *Primary muscle(s) affected: Latissimus dorsi. Position yourself on a pulldown machine and grasp a bar with a close grip with palms facing you and arms extended upward (first photo). Slowly pull the bar downward until the bar touches the midpoint of your chest (second photo). Pause, raise the bar, and repeat. Concentrate on pushing your elbows downward when pulling the bar to your chest.*

Exercise: Pulldown. *Primary muscle(s) affected: Latissimus dorsi. On a pull-down machine, grasp a bar with your palms facing away from your body and arms fully extended above your head (first photo). Slowly pull the bar downward until it touches the top portion of your chest (second photo). Pause, raise the bar, and repeat. Concentrate on pushing your elbows downward as you pull the bar toward your chest.*

Exercise: Chin-up. *Primary muscle(s) affected: Latissimus dorsi. Grasp an overhead bar with hands slightly less than shoulder width, your palms facing you, and arms fully extended (first photo). Pull your body upward until your chin is above the bar (second photo), pause, lower, and repeat. Concentrate on pushing your elbows downward while lifting your body upward.*

Exercise: Pull-up. *Primary muscle(s) affected: Latissimus dorsi. Grasp an overhead bar with hands more than shoulder width apart and facing away from you. Begin with arms fully extended (first photo). Pull your* *body upward until your chin is positioned above the bar (second photo). Pause, lower, and repeat. Concentrate on pushing your elbows downward while lifting your body upward.*

Exercise: Seated row. *Primary muscle(s) affected: Latissimus dorsi, iliocostalis lumborum (often referred to as a spinal erector). Sit on a seated row machine with slightly bent knees. Grasp a rowing handle at arms' length in front of your body, and lean as far forward as possible (first photo). Slowly lean back to a vertical posi-* *tion while you pull the handle to your lower stomach region (second photo). Pause, lean forward, extend your arms, and repeat. Concentrate on pushing your elbows backward while pulling the handle toward you. Keep your elbows close to your body.*

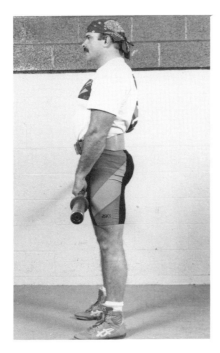

Exercise: Stiff-leg deadlift with a rounded back (standing). *Primary muscle(s) affected: Iliocostalis lomborum (spinal erector). Grasp a bar with a shoulder width grip and arms fully extended in front of your body and legs nearly locked (first photo). Slowly lower the bar toward the floor as far as possible while allowing your back to round out (second photo). Pause, rise upward, and repeat.*

Exercise: Stiff-leg deadlift with a rounded back (seated). *Primary muscle(s) affected: Iliocostalis lomborum (spinal erector). Sit on a seated row machine with legs nearly straight and while grasping a bar at arms' length in front of your body, lean as far forward as possi-* *ble (first photo). Slowly lean backward until in a lying position on your back (second photo). Pause, rise upward and forward, and repeat. Keep your arms extended throughout the entire movement.*

Exercise: Good mornings. *Primary muscle(s) affected: Iliocostalis lomborum (spinal erector). Position a bar on your shoulders, with legs straight and hands comfortably located on the bar (first photo). Slowly lower your chest toward the floor as far as possible (second photo). Pause, rise, and repeat. Do not arch back.*

Exercise: Pushdown. *Primary muscle(s) affected: Triceps. Grasp a bar connected to the cable of a high pulley with arms bent at 90 degrees at the elbow joint (first photo). Slowly extend your arms downward until straight (second photo). Pause, raise the bar to 90 degrees, and repeat. Keep your elbows close to your body at all times.*

Exercise: Close-grip bench press. *Primary muscle(s) affected: Triceps. Lying on your back on a bench, grasp a bar palms up, with hands approximately 10-12in apart. Slowly lower the bar to a point about 3-4in directly above*

your chest (first photo), then push the bar upward to arms' length (second photo) and repeat. Direct your elbows down toward your knees and close to your sides whenever possible.

Exercise: Seated French curl. *Primary muscle(s) affected: Triceps. Seated on a bench, grasp a single dumbbell beneath the head of the dumbbell, with both hands and arms bent at 90 degrees (first photo). Push the*

dumbbell upward while keeping your elbows forward, until your arms are fully extended above your head (second photo). Pause, lower, and repeat.

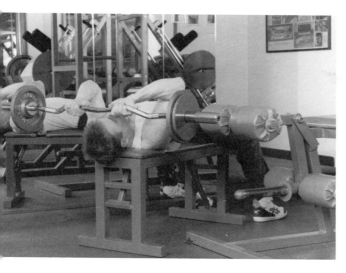

Exercise: Lying French curl. *Primary muscle(s) affected: Triceps. Lying face up on a bench, grasp a bar at less than shoulder width. Lower the bar within 2in of your forehead to begin the exercise (first photo)—arms should be slightly less than 90 degrees at the elbow joint. Slowly* *raise the bar upward, to arms' length, without moving your elbows (second photo). Pause, lower, and repeat. For more emphasis on your triceps, position your elbows forward throughout the movement.*

Exercise: Tricep dip. *Primary muscle(s) affected: Triceps. Supporting your body weight with your hands positioned on dip bars, begin with your arms bent roughly 90 degrees at the elbow joint (first photo). Keeping your head* *up and back arched, push your body upward until your arms are fully extended (second photo). Pause, lower, and repeat.*

Exercise: Standing bicep curl. *Primary muscle(s) affected: Biceps. Grasping a bar with palms up at about shoulder width, begin the movement with your arms fully extended (first photo). Slowly raise the bar until resistance starts to diminish (second photo). Pause, lower, and repeat. Keep your elbows close to your body without moving them forward.*

Exercise: Dumbbell curl. *Primary muscle(s) affected: Biceps. Seated or standing, grasp a dumbbell with your thumb forward, and arm fully extended downward (first photo). Raise the dumbbell upward as you rotate the forward head of the dumbbell outward. Stop the upward movement when resistance begins to decrease—do not curl the weight upward as far as possible (second photo). Pause, lower to arm's length, and repeat. Caution: Do not use your back to help raise the dumbbell.*

Exercise: Preacher curl. *Primary muscle(s) affected: Biceps. Positioned on a preacher curl bench, while holding a dumbbell, palm up, begin with your arm fully extended over the bench (first photo). Slowly curl the dumbbell upward, but stop shy of the point where resistance begins to reduce significantly (second photo). Pause, lower, and repeat. Be sure to keep your elbow anchored on the bench at all times.*

Exercise: Hammer curl. *Primary muscle(s) affected: Biceps, brachialis, brachioradialis. Seated or standing, grasp a dumbbell with thumb forward and arm slightly bent and hanging downward at your side (first photo). Slowly raise the weight upward while maintaining a thumbs-up position, until resistance reduces (second photo). Pause, lower, and repeat.*

Exercise: Reverse curl. *Primary muscle(s) affected: Biceps, brachialis, brachioradialis. Grasp a bar with palms toward you at roughly shoulder width and arms extended in front of you (first photo). Keeping your elbows close to your body, raise the bar upward as far as possible (second photo). Pause, lower, and repeat.*

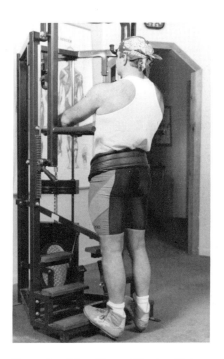

Exercise: *Standing calf raise. Primary muscle(s) affected: Gastrocnemius. Stand on a step or standing calf raise machine on the balls of your feet with heels hanging off the step. Lower your heels downward as far as is comfortable (first photo). Slowly rise up on the balls of your feet as far as possible (second photo). Pause, lower, and repeat. Hold on with your hands to maintain your balance.*

Exercise: Seated calf raise. *Primary muscle(s) affected: Soleus. Sit on a seated calf machine with heels lowered as far as possible toward the floor (first photo).*

Slowly push the balls of your feet downward while rising up on your toes as far as possible (second photo). Pause, lower, and repeat.

Exercise: *Wrist curl. Primary muscle(s) affected: Brachioradialis, flexor carpi radialis. In a standing or seated position, grasp a dumbbell in one hand with your thumb on the same side of the handle as your fingers, and your wrist fully extended (first photo). Slowly curl your wrist upward and toward your body as far as possible (second photo). Pause, lower, and repeat.*

Exercise: *Reverse crunch. Primary muscle(s) affected: Lower rectus abdominus (abdominals). Lie on your back with knees at 90 degrees and hands positioned out and to the side of your hips for support (first photo). Slowly rotate your hips toward your upper body as far as possible without raising your lower back off the floor (second photo). Pause, lower, and repeat. Tip: When you rotate your hips, force your lower back down against the floor. For increased resistance, straighten your legs some, but don't ever completely extend them.*

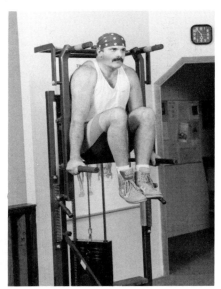

Exercise: Knee-up. *Primary muscle(s) affected: Lower rectus abdominus (abdominals). Position yourself on dip bars with fully extended arms and straight legs (first photo). Slowly bring your knees toward your chest as far as possible (second photo). Pause, lower, and repeat. As your knees move upward, lean your upper body forward and attempt to round out your back as much as you can. You may not be able to raise your knees very high, but remember—your abdominals flex your spine roughly 30 degrees, so the movement can be very limited but still effective.*

Exercise: Twisting crunch. *Primary muscle(s) affected: Internal and external obliques. Lie on your back with your feet near your buttocks and your hands together behind your head (first photo). As you tuck your chin, raise your right shoulder off the ground while directing your*

right elbow toward your left knee (second photo). Pause, lower, and repeat for the other side. As you raise upward, force your lower back down against the floor. Caution: Do not pull on your head with your hands.

Exercise: Roman chair crunch. *Primary muscle(s) affected: Upper rectus abdominus (abdominals). Position yourself on a Roman chair with your legs bent and buttocks located just off the pad (first photo). Tuck your chin*

and slowly crunch upward until resistance begins to cease (second photo). Pause, lower, and repeat. Remember, your abdominals only flex your spine, so the movement is small.

Exercise: Incline crunch. *Primary muscle(s) affected: Upper rectus abdominus (abdominals). Lie on an incline board with feet positioned higher than your shoulders and hands locked behind your head (first photo). Slowly raise your shoulders as far as possible upward, while* *tucking your chin and forcing your lower back down against the pad (second photo). Always keep your legs bent and direct your chin toward your navel when rising upward. Pause, lower, and repeat.*

Exercise: Rope pull. *Primary muscle(s) affected: Upper rectus abdominus (abdominals). Sit in an erect position and grasp a rope connected to a high pulley (first photo). Tuck your chin and direct your chin toward your navel while you round out your back as much as possible (second photo). Pause, rise upward, and repeat. Make sure to rise to an erect position before crunching downward.*

Chapter 8

Sample Workout Programs

*Those involved in this sport of speed and skill are only as good as their
efforts to keep their body healthy, fit, and injury-free.
When injuries do occur, it's crucial to take the appropriate scientific
measures to guarantee complete and speedy recovery.*

8.1 Specifically Designed Workouts

This chapter contains sample workouts based on time allotments, workout formats, and emphasis (for fitness enthusiasts, race drivers, pit crew members, or strength trainers). Keep in mind that these are only *samples,* not workouts written in stone. Rather, they serve as viable alternatives to your training. Each workout is designed for males. For female training alternatives, refer to the chart elsewhere in this book for appropriate recommended repetition ranges.

Total Body Workout, Two to Three Days Weekly

Exercise	General Conditioning Sets x Repetitions	Strength Training Sets x Repetitions
Squat or leg press	—	3 x 6-8
Leg extension	2 x 8-12	1 x 6-8
Leg curl	2 x 8-12	2 x 6-8
Bench press	—	2 x 6-8
Flye	2 x 8-12	2 x 6-8
Upright row	3 x 8-12	3 x 6-8
Pulldown	3 x 8-12	3 x 6-8
Seated row	2 x 8-12	2 x 6-8
Stiff-leg deadlift (back rounded)	—	2 x 6-8
Pushdown	3 x 8-12	2 x 6-8
Seated french curl	—	2 x 6-8
Dumbbell curl	3 x 8-12	2 x 6-8
Hammer curl	—	2 x 6-8
Standing calf raise	1 x 15-20	2 x 15-20
Abdominals	(see abdominal workout later in this chapter)	

Total Body Workout, Two to Three Days Weekly
Minimum requirements

Exercise	General Conditioning Sets x Repetitions	Strength Training Sets x Repetitions
Squat or leg press	1 x 8-12	1 x 6-8
Leg curl	1 x 8-12	1 x 6-8
Dumbbell bench press	1 x 8-12	1 x 6-8
Upright row	1 x 8-12	1 x 6-8
Pulldown	1 x 8-12	1 x 6-8
Seated row	1 x 8-12	1 x 6-8
Pushdown	1 x 8-12	1 x 6-8
Standing bicep curl	1 x 8-12	1 x 6-8
Standing calf raise	1 x 15-20	1 x 15-20
Abdominals	(see abdominal workout later in this chapter)	

Total Body Workout, Two to Three Days Weekly
Emphasis: Pit crew

Exercise	General Conditioning Sets x Repetitions	Strength Training Sets x Repetitions
Squat or leg press	3 x 8-12	3 x 6-8
Leg extension	2 x 8-12	2 x 6-8
Stiff-leg deadlift (back arched)	3 x 8-12	3 x 6-8
Dumbbell bench press	3 x 8-12	3 x 6-8
Flye	2 x 8-12	2 x 6-8
Front deltoid raise	3 x 8-12	3 x 6-8
Lateral raise	2 x 8-12	2 x 6-8
Bent-over lateral raise	2 x 8-12	2 x 6-8
Shoulder shrugs	3 x 8-12	3 x 6-8
Pulldown	2 x 8-12	2 x 6-8
Seated row	2 x 8-12	2 x 6-8
Good mornings	2 x 8-12	2 x 6-8
Pushdown	2 x 8-12	2 x 6-8
Tricep dips	2 x 8-12	2 x 6-8
Dumbbell curl	2 x 8-12	2 x 6-8
Hammer curl	3 x 8-12	3 x 6-8
Standing calf raise	2 x 15-20	2 x 15-20
Wrist curl	2 x 8-12	2 x 6-8
Abdominals	(see abdominal workout later in this chapter)	

Total Body Workout, Two to Three Days Weekly
Emphasis: Driver

Exercise	General Conditioning Sets x Repetitions	Strength Training Sets x Repetitions
Squat or leg press	3 x 8-12	3 x 6-8
Leg extension	2 x 8-12	2 x 6-8
Stiff-leg deadlift (back arched)	4 x 8-12	4 x 6-8
Dumbbell bench press	2 x 8-12	2 x 6-8
Pec deck	3 x 8-12	3 x 6-8
Front deltoid raise	2 x 8-12	2 x 6-8
Upright row	3 x 8-12	3 x 6-8
Shoulder shrugs	3 x 8-12	3 x 6-8
Pull-ups	3 x 8-12	3 x 6-8
Seated row	2 x 8-12	2 x 6-8
Stiff-leg deadlift (back rounded)	3 x 8-12	3 x 6-8
Pushdown	3 x 8-12	3 x 6-8
Lying french curl	2 x 8-12	2 x 6-8
Preacher curl	2 x 8-12	2 x 6-8
Hammer curl	3 x 8-12	3 x 6-8
Standing calf raise	2 x 15-20	2 x 15-20
Seated calf raise	2 x 15-20	2 x 15-20
Wrist curl	2 x 8-12	2 x 6-8
Abdominals	(see abdominal workout later in this chapter)	

Total Body Workout Three Days Weekly
Circuit-training regimen 1
Remember: Take a rest time of only 15-30sec between exercises during circuit training.

Exercise	General Conditioning Sets x Repetitions	Strength Training Sets x Repetitions
Leg press	1 x 8-12	1 x 6-8
Leg curl	1 x 8-12	1 x 6-8
Leg extension	1 x 8-12	1 x 6-8
Dumbbell bench press	1 x 8-12	1 x 6-8
Chest dips	1 x 8-12	1 x 6-8
Front deltoid raise	1 x 8-12	1 x 6-8
Lateral raise	1 x 8-12	1 x 6-8
Bent-over lateral raise	1 x 8-12	1 x 6-8
Pulldown	1 x 8-12	1 x 6-8
Seated row	1 x 8-12	1 x 6-8
Stiff-leg deadlift (back rounded)	1 x 8-12	1 x 6-8
Tricep dips	1 x 8-12	1 x 6-8
Pushdown	1 x 8-12	1 x 6-8
Standing bicep curl	1 x 8-12	1 x 6-8
Reverse curl	1 x 8-12	1 x 6-8
Standing calf raise	1 x 15-20	1 x 15-20
Wrist curl	1 x 8-12	1 x 6-8
Abdominals	(see abdominal workout later in this chapter)	

Total Body Workout Three Days Weekly
Circuit-training regimen 2
Exercises in this workout are organized to allow each muscle group to recover somewhat, during which time another muscle group is worked. Then you return to the original muscle group to work another type of exercise.

Exercise	General Conditioning Sets x Repetitions	Strength Training Sets x Repetitions
Leg press	1 x 8-12	1 x 6-8
Dumbbell bench press	1 x 8-12	1 x 6-8
Leg curl	1 x 8-12	1 x 6-8
Chest dips	1 x 8-12	1 x 6-8
Leg extension	1 x 8-12	1 x 6-8
Front deltoid raise	1 x 8-12	1 x 6-8
Pulldown	1 x 8-12	1 x 6-8
Lateral raise	1 x 8-12	1 x 6-8
Seated row	1 x 8-12	1 x 6-8
Bent-over lateral raise	1 x 8-12	1 x 6-8
Stiff-leg deadlift (back rounded)	1 x 8-12	1 x 6-8
Tricep dips	1 x 8-12	1 x 6-8
Standing bicep curl	1 x 8-12	1 x 6-8
Pushdown	1 x 8-12	1 x 6-8
Reverse curl	1 x 8-12	1 x 6-8
Standing calf raise	1 x 15-20	1 x 15-20
Wrist curl	1 x 8-12	1 x 6-8
Abdominals	(see abdominal workout	

Total Body Workout Three Days Weekly
Circuit-training regimen 3

This sample circuit-training program is, for the most part, designed around working opposing muscle groups. For instance, while working your upper arms you can perform a bicep exercise, then a tricep exercise, and then repeat the sequence for the appropriate number of sets and exercises per muscle group.

Exercise	General Conditioning Sets x Repetitions	Strength Training Sets x Repetitions
Leg press	1 x 8-12	1 x 6-8
Leg curl	1 x 8-12	1 x 6-8
Leg extension	1 x 8-12	1 x 6-8
Stiff-leg deadlift (back arched)	1 x 8-12	1 x 6-8
Bench press	1 x 8-12	1 x 6-8
Pulldown	1 x 8-12	1 x 6-8
Dumbbell bench press	1 x 8-12	1 x 6-8
Seated row	1 x 8-12	1 x 6-8
Front deltoid raise	1 x 8-12	1 x 6-8
Bent-over lateral raise	1 x 8-12	1 x 6-8
Upright row	1 x 8-12	1 x 6-8
Reverse-grip pulldown	1 x 8-12	1 x 6-8
Good mornings	1 x 8-12	1 x 6-8
Abdominals	(see abdominal workout later in this chapter)	
Pushdown	1 x 8-12	1 x 6-8
Dumbbell curl	1 x 8-12	1 x 6-8
Lying french curl	1 x 8-12	1 x 6-8
Standing bicep curl	1 x 8-12	1 x 6-8
Standing calf raise	1 x 15-20	1 x 15-20
Hammer curl	1 x 8-12	1 x 6-8
Wrist curl	1 x 8-12	1 x 6-8

Two-Day Split Routine, Four to Six Days Weekly

When you can devote at least four days a week to exercise, it is best to follow a two-day split routine. That is, one workout for selected muscle groups and another for the remaining muscle groups. This allows you to perform additional sets of exercises per body part without increasing the length of your workout sessions.

Exercise	General Conditioning Sets x Repetitions	Strength Training Sets x Repetitions
Day #1		
Squat or leg press	3 x 8-12	4 x 6-8
Leg extension	3 x 8-12	3 x 6-8
Dumbbell bench press	3 x 8-12	4 x 6-8
Flye	3 x 8-12	3 x 6-8
Overhead press	3 x 8-12	3 x 6-8
Lateral raise	3 x 8-12	3 x 6-8
Bent-over lateral raise	3 x 8-12	3 x 6-8
Shoulder shrugs	3 x 8-12	3 x 6-8
Seated french curl	4 x 8-12	4 x 6-8
Tricep dips	3 x 8-12	3 x 6-8
Abdominals	(see abdominal workout later in this chapter)	
Day #2		
Leg curl	3 x 8-12	3 x 6-8
Stiff-leg deadlift (back arched)	4 x 8-12	4 x 6-8
Chin-ups	3 x 8-12	3 x 6-8
Pull-ups	3 x 8-12	3 x 6-8
Seated row	3 x 8-12	3 x 6-8
Good mornings	3 x 8-12	3 x 6-8
Dumbbell curl	3 x 8-12	3 x 6-8
Preacher curl	3 x 8-12	3 x 6-8
Reverse curl	3 x 8-12	3 x 6-8
Standing calf raise	3 x 15-20	3 x 15-20
Wrist curl	3 x 8-12	3 x 6-8
Abdominals	(see abdominal workout later in this chapter)	

Two-Day Split Routine, Four to Six Days Weekly
Minimum requirements

Exercise	General Conditioning Sets x Repetitions	Strength Training Sets x Repetitions
Day #1		
Squat or leg press	2 x 8-12	2 x 6-8
Leg extension	2 x 8-12	2 x 6-8
Leg curl	2 x 8-12	2 x 6-8
Stiff-leg deadlift (back arched)	2 x 8-12	2 x 6-8
Standing calf raise	1 x 15-20	1 x 15-20
Abdominals	(see abdominal workout later in this chapter)	
Day #2		
Dumbbell bench press	2 x 8-12	2 x 6-8
Upright row	2 x 8-12	2 x 6-8
Pulldown	2 x 8-12	2 x 6-8
Seated row	2 x 8-12	2 x 6-8
Good mornings	2 x 8-12	2 x 6-8
Pushdown	2 x 8-12	2 x 6-8
Standing bicep curl	2 x 8-12	2 x 6-8
Hammer curl	2 x 8-12	2 x 6-8
Abdominals	(see abdominal workout later in this chapter)	

Two-Day Split Routine, Four to Six Days Weekly
Emphasis: Pit crew

Exercise	General Conditioning Sets x Repetitions	Strength Training Sets x Repetitions
Day #1		
Bench press	2 x 8-12	2 x 6-8
Dumbbell bench press	3 x 8-12	3 x 6-8
Stiff-leg deadlift (back arched)	4 x 8-12	4 x 6-8
Front deltoid raise	3 x 8-12	3 x 6-8
Lateral raise	3 x 8-12	3 x 6-8
Bent-over lateral raise	2 x 8-12	2 x 6-8
Shoulder shrugs	3 x 8-12	2 x 6-8
Pushdown	2 x 8-12	2 x 6-8
Tricep dips	3 x 8-12	3 x 6-8
Standing calf raise	3 x 15-20	3 x 15-20
Abdominals	(see abdominal workout later in this chapter)	

Day #2

Exercise	General Conditioning Sets x Repetitions	Strength Training Sets x Repetitions
Squat or leg press	4 x 8-12	4 x 6-8
Leg extension	2 x 8-12	2 x 6-8
Reverse-grip pulldown	2 x 8-12	2 x 6-8
Pulldown	2 x 8-12	2 x 6-8
Seated row	2 x 8-12	2 x 6-8
Good mornings	4 x 8-12	4 x 6-8
Dumbbell curl	2 x 8-12	2 x 6-8
Hammer curl	3 x 8-12	3 x 6-8
Wrist curl	3 x 8-12	3 x 6-8
Abdominals	(see abdominal workout later in this chapter)	

Two-Day Split Routine, Four to Six Days Weekly
Emphasis: Driver

Exercise	General Conditioning Sets x Repetitions	Strength Training Sets x Repetitions
Day #1		
Squat or leg press	2 x 8-12	2 x 6-8
Leg extension	2 x 8-12	2 x 6-8
Leg curl	2 x 8-12	2 x 6-8
Stiff-leg deadlift (back arched)	4 x 8-12	4 x 6-8
Reverse-grip pulldown	2 x 8-12	2 x 6-8
Pulldown	2 x 8-12	2 x 6-8
Seated row	2 x 8-12	2 x 6-8
Good mornings	4 x 8-12	4 x 6-8
Standing calf raise	3 x 15-20	3 x 15-20
Seated calf raise	3 x 15-20	3 x 15-20
Abdominals	(see abdominal workout later in this chapter)	
Day #2		
Bench press	3 x 8-12	3 x 6-8
Dumbbell bench press	2 x 8-12	2 x 6-8
Overhead press	3 x 8-12	3 x 6-8
Upright row	3 x 8-12	3 x 6-8
Bent-over lateral raise	2 x 8-12	2 x 6-8
Shoulder shrugs	3 x 8-12	3 x 6-8
Pushdown	2 x 8-12	2 x 6-8
Seated French curl	3 x 8-12	3 x 6-8
Dumbbell curl	3 x 8-12	3 x 6-8
Hammer curl	3 x 8-12	3 x 6-8
Wrist curl	3 x 8-12	3 x 6-8
Abdominals	(see abdominal workout later in this chapter)	

Two-Day Split Routine–Integrated Training (in the Same Workout), Four to Six Days Weekly

Emphasis: Driver

Here is a sample of an integrated strength and power-speed training program. In order to protect against injury, you need an established foundation of strength before attempting any power-speed training. This can mean four weeks of strength training before following this program. Since strength and power-speed training require such heavy workouts, we recommend a program like this to be followed for no more than four to six weeks. In addition, you can select any two training formats for program design.

Exercise	Sets x Repetitions
Day #1	
Squat or leg press	2 x 3-5, 1 x 6-8
Leg extension	2 x 6-8
Leg curl	2 x 6-8
Stiff-leg deadlift (back arched)	3 x 3-5, 1 x 6-8
Reverse-grip pulldown	2 x 3-5
Pulldown	2 x 6-8
Seated row	2 x 6-8
Good mornings	3 x 3-5, 1 x 6-8
Standing calf raise	3 x 15-20
Seated calf raise	3 x 15-20
Abdominals	(see abdominal workout later in this chapter)
Day #2	
Bench press	3 x 3-5, 1 x 6-8
Dumbbell bench press	2 x 6-8
Overhead press	2 x 3-5, 1 x 6-8
Upright row	3 x 6-8
Bent-over lateral raise	2 x 6-8
Shoulder shrugs	3 x 6-8
Pushdown	2 x 3-5
Seated French curl	3 x 6-8
Dumbbell curl	2 x 3-5, 1 x 6-8
Hammer curl	3 x 6-8
Wrist curl	3 x 6-8
Abdominals	(see abdominal workout later in this chapter)

Two-Day Split Routine–Integrated Training (on Separate Workout Days), Four to Six Days Weekly

The following chart is a sample of an integrated muscle hypertrophy program. One workout is designed for muscle enlargement of slow-twitch muscle fibers while the other is designed for stressing the fast-twitch fibers. Simply alternate the workouts throughout your total exercise regimen.

Although the recommended repetition range for hypertrophy of slow-twitch muscle fibers is fifteen to forty, we have followed recommendations of fifteen to twenty for time-saving purposes only.

Exercise	Fast-Twitch Fibers Sets x Repetitions	Slow-Twitch Fibers Sets x Repetitions
Day #1		
Bench press	3 x 8-12	3 x 15-20
Flye	2 x 8-12	3 x 15-20
Front deltoid raise	2 x 8-12	2 x 15-20
Lateral raise	2 x 8-12	2 x 15-20
Bent-over lateral raise	2 x 8-12	2 x 15-20
Shoulder shrugs	3 x 8-12	3 x 15-20
Lying French curl	2 x 8-12	2 x 15-20
Tricep dips	2 x 8-12	2 x 15-20
Wrist curl	2 x 8-12	2 x 15-20
Standing calf raise	2 x 15-20	2 x 15-20
Day #2		
Squat or leg press	3 x 8-12	3 x 15-20
Leg extension	2 x 8-12	2 x 15-20
Leg curl	2 x 8-12	2 x 15-20
Stiff-leg deadlift (back arched)	3 x 8-12	3 x 15-20
Pulldown	2 x 8-12	2 x 15-20
Seated row	2 x 8-12	2 x 15-20
Good mornings	2 x 8-12	2 x 15-20
Standing bicep curl	2 x 8-12	2 x 15-20
Dumbbell curl	2 x 8-12	2 x 15-20
Hammer curl	2 x 8-12	2 x 15-20
Abdominals	(see abdominal workout later in this chapter)	

Three-Day Split Routine #1, Five to Six Days Weekly

When you can dedicate five to six days a week to exercise, it is best to follow a three-day split routine. That is, one workout for selected muscle group, a second for other selected muscle groups, and a third for the remaining muscle groups. This allows you to perform a larger volume of work using an increased number of sets and exercises per body part without appreciably increasing the length of each workout session.

| | General Conditioning | Strength Training |
	Sets x Repetitions	Sets x Repetitions
Exercise		
Day #1		
Bench press	3 x 8-12	3 x 6-8
Dumbbell bench press	2 x 8-12	2 x 6-8
Crossover	3 x 8-12	3 x 6-8
Overhead press	3 x 8-12	3 x 6-8
Lateral raise	3 x 8-12	3 x 6-8
Bent-over lateral raise	3 x 8-12	3 x 6-8
Shoulder shrugs	3 x 8-12	3 x 6-8
Pushdown	3 x 8-12	3 x 6-8
Seated French curl	3 x 8-12	3 x 6-8
Lying French curl	3 x 8-12	3 x 6-8
Abdominals	(see abdominal workout later in this chapter)	
Day #2		
Leg curl	3 x 8-12	3 x 6-8
Stiff-leg deadlift (back arched)	3 x 8-12	3 x 6-8
Chin-ups	3 x 8-12	3 x 6-8
Pull-ups	3 x 8-12	3 x 6-8
Seated row	3 x 8-12	3 x 6-8
Good mornings	3 x 8-12	3 x 6-8
Standing bicep curl	3 x 8-12	3 x 6-8
Dumbbell curl	3 x 8-12	3 x 6-8
Preacher curl	3 x 8-12	3 x 6-8
Hammer curl	3 x 8-12	3 x 6-8
Day #3		
Squat	3 x 8-12	3 x 6-8
Leg press	3 x 8-12	3 x 6-8
Leg extension	3 x 8-12	3 x 6-8
Standing calf raise	3 x 15-20	3 x 15-20
Wrist curl	3 x 8-12	3 x 6-8
Abdominals	(see abdominal workout later in this chapter)	

Three-Day Split Routine #2, Five or Six Days Weekly

| | General Conditioning | Strength Training |
	Sets x Repetitions	Sets x Repetitions
Exercise		
Day #1		
Bench press	3 x 8-12	3 x 6-8
Flye	3 x 8-12	3 x 6-8
Chest dips	3 x 8-12	3 x 6-8
Reverse-grip pulldown	3 x 8-12	3 x 6-8
Pulldown	3 x 8-12	3 x 6-8
Seated row	3 x 8-12	3 x 6-8
Stiff-leg deadlift (back rounded)	3 x 8-12	3 x 6-8
Dumbbell curl	3 x 8-12	3 x 6-8
Preacher curl	3 x 8-12	3 x 6-8
Reverse curl	3 x 8-12	3 x 6-8
Day #2		
Front deltoid raise	3 x 8-12	3 x 6-8
Lateral raise	3 x 8-12	3 x 6-8
Bent-over lateral raise	3 x 8-12	3 x 6-8
Shoulder shrugs	3 x 8-12	3 x 6-8
Seated French curl	3 x 8-12	3 x 6-8
Lying French curl	3 x 8-12	3 x 6-8
Tricep dips	3 x 8-12	3 x 6-8
Wrist curl	3 x 8-12	3 x 6-8
Abdominals	(see abdominal workout later in this chapter)	
Day #3		
Squat	3 x 8-12	3 x 6-8
Leg press	3 x 8-12	3 x 6-8
Leg extension	3 x 8-12	3 x 6-8
Leg curl	3 x 8-12	3 x 6-8
Stiff-leg deadlift (back arched)	3 x 8-12	3 x 6-8
Standing calf raise	3 x 15-20	3 x 15-20
Abdominals	(see abdominal workout later in this chapter)	

Three-Day Split Routine #3, Five to Six Days Weekly

Exercise	General Conditioning Sets x Repetitions	Strength Training Sets x Repetitions
Day #1		
Bench press	3 x 8-12	3 x 6-8
Dumbbell bench press	3 x 8-12	3 x 6-8
Pec deck	3 x 8-12	3 x 6-8
Overhead press	3 x 8-12	3 x 6-8
Upright row	3 x 8-12	3 x 6-8
Bent-over lateral raise	3 x 8-12	3 x 6-8
Shoulder shrugs	3 x 8-12	3 x 6-8
Standing calf raise	3 x 15-20	3 x 15-20
Abdominals	(see abdominal workout later in this chapter)	
Day #2		
Chin-ups	3 x 8-12	3 x 6-8
Pulldown	3 x 8-12	3 x 6-8
Seated row	3 x 8-12	3 x 6-8
Good mornings	3 x 8-12	3 x 6-8
Leg curl	3 x 8-12	3 x 6-8
Stiff-leg deadlift (back arched)	3 x 8-12	3 x 6-8
Tricep dips	3 x 8-12	3 x 6-8
Seated French curl	3 x 8-12	3 x 6-8
Lying French curl	3 x 8-12	3 x 6-8
Day #3		
Squat	3 x 8-12	3 x 6-8
Leg press	3 x 8-12	3 x 6-8
Leg extension	3 x 8-12	3 x 6-8
Standing bicep curl	3 x 8-12	3 x 6-8
Dumbbell curl	3 x 8-12	3 x 6-8
Hammer curl	3 x 8-12	3 x 6-8
Reverse curl	3 x 8-12	3 x 6-8
Wrist curl	3 x 8-12	3 x 6-8
Abdominals	(see abdominal workout later in this chapter)	

Three-Day Split Routine Five or Six Days Weekly
Minimum requirements 1

Exercise	General Conditioning Sets x Repetitions	Strength Training Sets x Repetitions
Day #1		
Bench press	2 x 8-12	2 x 6-8
Flye	2 x 8-12	2 x 6-8
Overhead press	2 x 8-12	2 x 6-8
Upright row	2 x 8-12	2 x 6-8
Shoulder shrugs	2 x 8-12	2 x 6-8
Lying French curl	2 x 8-12	2 x 6-8
Tricep dips	2 x 8-12	2 x 6-8
Abdominals	(see abdominal workout later in this chapter)	
Day #2		
Leg curl	2 x 8-12	2 x 6-8
Stiff-leg deadlift (back arched)	2 x 8-12	2 x 6-8
Pulldown	2 x 8-12	2 x 6-8
Seated row	2 x 8-12	2 x 6-8
Good mornings	2 x 8-12	2 x 6-8
Standing bicep curl	2 x 8-12	2 x 6-8
Reverse curl	2 x 8-12	2 x 6-8
Day #3		
Squat or leg press	3 x 8-12	3 x 6-8
Leg extension	2 x 8-12	2 x 6-8
Standing calf raise	1 x 15-20	1 x 15-20
Wrist curl	2 x 8-12	2 x 6-8
Abdominals	(see abdominal workout later in this chapter)	

Three-Day Split Routine Five or Six Days Weekly
Minimum requirements 2

Exercise	General Conditioning Sets x Repetitions	Strength Training Sets x Repetitions
Day #1		
Bench press	3 x 8-12	3 x 6-8
Dumbbell bench press	2 x 8-12	2 x 6-8
Pulldown	3 x 8-12	3 x 6-8
Seated row	2 x 8-12	2 x 6-8
Stiff-leg deadlift (back rounded)	3 x 8-12	3 x 6-8
Preacher curl	3 x 8-12	3 x 6-8
Reverse curl	3 x 8-12	3 x 6-8
Day #2		
Front deltoid raise	2 x 8-12	2 x 6-8
Upright row	2 x 8-12	2 x 6-8
Shoulder shrugs	3 x 8-12	3 x 6-8
Seated French curl	2 x 8-12	2 x 6-8
Pushdown	2 x 8-12	2 x 6-8
Wrist curl	2 x 8-12	2 x 6-8
Abdominals	(see abdominal workout later in this chapter)	
Day #3		
Leg press	3 x 8-12	3 x 6-8
Leg extension	2 x 8-12	2 x 6-8
Stiff-leg deadlift (back arched)	3 x 8-12	3 x 6-8
Standing calf raise	1 x 15-20	1 x 15-20
Abdominals	(see abdominal workout later in this chapter)	

Three-Day Split Routine, Five or Six Days Weekly
Emphasis: Pit crew

Exercise	General Conditioning Sets x Repetitions	Strength Training Sets x Repetitions
Day #1		
Bench press	3 x 8-12	3 x 6-8
Flye	3 x 8-12	3 x 6-8
Chest dips	2 x 8-12	2 x 6-8
Pulldown	2 x 8-12	2 x 6-8
Seated row	3 x 8-12	3 x 6-8
Stiff-leg deadlift (back rounded)	4 x 8-12	4 x 6-8
Lying French curl	2 x 8-12	2 x 6-8
Tricep dips	3 x 8-12	3 x 6-8
Day #2		
Squat	3 x 8-12	3 x 6-8
Leg press	3 x 8-12	3 x 6-8
Leg extension	2 x 8-12	2 x 6-8
Front deltoid raise	3 x 8-12	3 x 6-8
Lateral raise	2 x 8-12	2 x 6-8
Bent-over lateral raise	2 x 8-12	2 x 6-8
Shoulder shrugs	3 x 8-12	3 x 6-8
Abdominals	(see abdominal workout later in this chapter)	
Day #3		
Leg curl	2 x 8-12	2 x 6-8
Stiff-leg deadlift (back arched)	4 x 8-12	4 x 6-8
Dumbbell curl	3 x 8-12	3 x 6-8
Preacher curl	2 x 8-12	2 x 6-8
Hammer curl	3 x 8-12	3 x 6-8
Wrist curl	3 x 8-12	3 x 6-8
Standing calf raise	3 x 15-20	3 x 15-20
Abdominals	(see abdominal workout later in this chapter)	

Three-Day Split Routine, Five or Six Days Weekly
Emphasis: Driver

Exercise	General Conditioning Sets x Repetitions	Strength Training Sets x Repetitions
Day #1		
Dumbbell bench press	3 x 8-12	3 x 6-8
Flye	2 x 8-12	2 x 6-8
Crossover	2 x 8-12	2 x 6-8
Overhead press	3 x 8-12	3 x 6-8
Upright row	3 x 8-12	3 x 6-8
Shoulder shrugs	4 x 8-12	4 x 6-8
Lying French curl	2 x 8-12	2 x 6-8
Tricep dips	3 x 8-12	3 x 6-8
Abdominals	(see abdominal workout later in this chapter)	

Exercise	General Conditioning Sets x Repetitions	Strength Training Sets x Repetitions
Day #2		
Leg curl	3 x 8-12	3 x 6-8
Stiff-leg deadlift (back arched)	3 x 8-12	3 x 6-8
Chin-ups	3 x 8-12	3 x 6-8
Pulldown	3 x 8-12	3 x 6-8
Seated row	2 x 8-12	2 x 6-8
Good mornings	4 x 8-12	4 x 6-8
Dumbbell curl	2 x 8-12	2 x 6-8
Preacher curl	2 x 8-12	2 x 6-8
Hammer curl	3 x 8-12	3 x 6-8
Day #3		
Squat or leg press	3 x 8-12	3 x 6-8
Leg extension	3 x 8-12	3 x 6-8
Standing calf raise	2 x 15-20	2 x 15-20
Seated calf raise	2 x 15-20	2 x 15-20
Wrist curl	3 x 8-12	3 x 6-8
Abdominals	(see abdominal workout later in this chapter)	

Four-Day Split Routine #1, Six Days Weekly
Off-season only

During the racing off-season, or when you are able to devote a full six days to exercise training, a four-day split routine may be just for you. The key here is to approach overtraining during each workout. That's why you not only work at a high intensity, but you also perform a large volume of work. Then the extra time allowed between workouts of the same muscle group is needed to ensure complete recovery.

Exercise	General Conditioning Sets x Repetitions	Strength Training Sets x Repetitions
Day #1		
Bench press	3 x 8-12	3 x 6-8
Pec deck	3 x 8-12	3 x 6-8
Crossover	3 x 8-12	3 x 6-8
Chest dips	3 x 8-12	3 x 6-8
Pushdown	3 x 8-12	3 x 6-8
Seated French curl	3 x 8-12	3 x 6-8
Lying French curl	3 x 8-12	3 x 6-8
Tricep dips	3 x 8-12	3 x 6-8
Day #2		
Leg curl	3 x 8-12	3 x 6-8
Stiff-leg deadlift (back arched)	3 x 8-12	3 x 6-8
Chin-ups	3 x 8-12	3 x 6-8
Pull-ups	3 x 8-12	3 x 6-8
Seated row	3 x 8-12	3 x 6-8
Good mornings	3 x 8-12	3 x 6-8
Standing calf raise	3 x 15-20	3 x 15-20
Seated calf raise	3 x 15-20	3 x 15-20
Abdominals	(see abdominal workout later in this chapter)	

Day #3

Overhead press	3 x 8-12	3 x 6-8
Lateral raise	3 x 8-12	3 x 6-8
Bent-over lateral raise	3 x 8-12	3 x 6-8
Shoulder shrugs	3 x 8-12	3 x 6-8
Dumbbell curl	3 x 8-12	3 x 6-8
Preacher curl	3 x 8-12	3 x 6-8
Hammer curl	3 x 8-12	3 x 6-8
Reverse curl	3 x 8-12	3 x 6-8

Day #4

Squat	3 x 8-12	3 x 6-8
Leg press	3 x 8-12	3 x 6-8
Leg extension	3 x 8-12	3 x 6-8
Wrist curl	3 x 8-12	3 x 6-8
Abdominals	(see abdominal workout later in this chapter)	

Four-Day Split Routine #2, Six Days Weekly

Off-season only

Exercise	General Conditioning Sets x Repetitions	Strength Training Sets x Repetitions
Day #1		
Bench press	4 x 8-12	4 x 6-8
Flye	4 x 8-12	4 x 6-8
Pec deck	4 x 8-12	4 x 6-8
Reverse-grip pulldown	4 x 8-12	4 x 6-8
Pulldown	4 x 8-12	4 x 6-8
Seated row	4 x 8-12	4 x 6-8
Stiff-leg deadlift (back rounded)	4 x 8-12	4 x 6-8
Day #2		
Squat or leg press	5 x 8-12	5 x 6-8
Leg extension	3 x 8-12	3 x 6-8
Standing bicep curl	3 x 8-12	3 x 6-8
Preacher curl	3 x 8-12	3 x 6-8
Hammer curl	4 x 8-12	4 x 6-8
Standing calf raise	3 x 15-20	3 x 15-20
Abdominals	(see abdominal workout later in this chapter)	
Day #3		
Overhead press	4 x 8-12	4 x 6-8
Lateral raise	4 x 8-12	4 x 6-8
Bent-over lateral raise	4 x 8-12	4 x 6-8
Shoulder shrugs	4 x 8-12	4 x 6-8
Seated French curl	4 x 8-12	4 x 6-8
Lying French curl	4 x 8-12	4 x 6-8
Tricep dips	4 x 8-12	4 x 6-8
Day #4		
Leg curl	3 x 8-12	3 x 6-8
Stiff-leg deadlift (back arched)	5 x 8-12	5 x 6-8
Wrist curl	4 x 8-12	4 x 6-8
Abdominals	(see abdominal workout later in this chapter)	

Abdominal Workout, Three to Five Days Weekly

To ensure total midsection muscle strength and tone, perform both lower abdominal exercises listed in section A, one oblique exercise from section B, and two exercises for the upper abdominals from section C. These exercises should be performed in a circuit type manner in the proper sequence (as listed from top to bottom), with no more than five seconds' rest between exercises. Remember, when you can perform twenty repetitions in good strict form, you need to make the exercise more difficult. Also keep in mind that your abdominal muscles flex (or bend) your spine forward, they don't bend you forward at your hips. Therefore, the movements involved in abdominal exercise are very limited in the possible range of motion.

A Lower abdominal muscles	Sets x Repetitions
Reverse crunch	1-2 x 15-20
Knee-up	1-2 x 15-20
B Oblique muscles	
Twisting crunch	1-2 x 15-20
Crunch with knees to side	1-2 x 15-20
C Upper abdominal muscles	
Roman chair crunch	1-2 x 15-20
Incline crunch	1-2 x 15-20
Rope pull	1-2 x 15-20

8.2 Selected Rehabilitation Workouts

The severity and type of injury you incur determines when rehabilitation can begin, especially that of resistance rehabilitation training. However, there are certain therapeutic measures you can take before beginning and during any resistance rehabilitation.

The first form of therapy is commonly referred to as RICE; R for rest, I for ice, C for compression, and E for elevation. RICE is normally recommended for the initial 48hr period following the time of the injury. These measures reduce swelling that occurs as a result of injuring various bodily tissues. By limiting the swelling, you lessen the chances of further damage to the tissues and allow the healing process to begin sooner.

A second form of rehabilitation is heat therapy. As we have stressed throughout this text, recovery is enhanced by an increase in blood flow to tissues damaged either during exercise or during the healing process following injury. Since the blood delivers nutrients necessary for the rebuilding and repair processes, an increase in tissue blood supply is needed to reduce recovery times.

Heat does just that. The subsequent rise in tissue temperatures from heat treatments causes a subsequent increase in blood flow to the underlying tissues. Heat, however, should *not* be used within the initial 48hr of an injury.

Ice therapy is a third option. Unbeknown to most people, the use of ice is not only beneficial immediately after being injured, it is also extremely beneficial at other times. Whenever the injured body part is used, whether it be during exercise, work, racing, or even massage, ice therapy is beneficial to the soft tissues (muscles, tendons, ligaments, and connective tissues) immediately afterward. Such therapy reduces muscle spasms; reduces inflammation and swelling that occurs after use; increases the pain threshold and thus reduces sensations of pain; and provides increased blood flow following removal of the cold. The latter benefit is little known and seldom practiced by many sports medicine personnel. Yet it's true that when cold treatments are removed, the body increases blood flow to the area in order to maintain normal tissue temperatures. And we all know the benefits of increased blood flow to the healing process.

Electrical Muscle Stimulation (EMS) allows you to stimulate your muscles to contract involuntarily (without the command from your brain) by means of electrical current. This is beneficial after exercise to help relax your muscles and reduce the chances of muscle spasms that can occur as a result of intense muscular contractions. In addition, the use of EMS promotes recovery by increasing the blood flow to the connected muscles. If an injury requires immobilization of a body part, EMS at least can help to maintain some associated nerve and muscle function that would otherwise be lost.

When pain is significantly reduced after an injury, stretching is the *first* means of rehabilitation. Not only can stretching increase blood flow to the injured tissues, but it also helps to reduce muscular tension that often accompanies injury.

As soon as a complete range of motion is attained without pain, resistance rehabilitation training should begin. We recommend that you stretch an injured body part before and after any rehabilitation exercise.

What follows are selected resistance rehabilitation workouts, along with recommended stretches. You can refer to chapter 7 for illustrations and explanations of the stretches and exercises. A table in chapter 5 lists recommendations on how hard you should work during your rehabilitation training.

Rehabilitation training should be practiced at least three days a week in addition to the training of uninjured body parts. *Remember:* Perform one set of each exercise during the first week of resistance rehabilitation training, two sets in the second week, and if no problems occur, three sets beginning week three. Attempt to carry each repetition throughout as full a range of motion as possible, but *do not work through pain!*

Rehabilitation Workout: Shoulder Injury

Stretches:
Spider walk up wall
Shoulder stretch
Arm across chest stretch
Shoulder to wall stretch

Exercises:	Sets x Repetitions
Front deltoid raise	1-3 x 15-40
Lateral raise (when possible)	1-3 x 15-40
Bent-over lateral raise	1-3 x 15-40
Shoulder shrugs	1-3 x 15-40

Exercises to do cautiously (may need to use very light weights):
Squat
Bench press
Dumbbell bench press
Overhead press
Upright row
Bent-over row

Rehabilitation Workout: Rib Injury

Stretches:
Spinal push-up
Hang from bar (when possible)

Exercises:	Sets x Repetitions
Crunches	1-3 x 15-40
Reverse-grip pulldown	1-3 x 15-40
Pulldown	1-3 x 15-40
Seated row	1-3 x 15-40
Flyes (when possible)	1-3 x 15-40

Exercises to do cautiously (may need to use very light weights):
Squat
Stiff-leg deadlift(s)
Dip(s)
Upright row
Chin-ups
Pull-ups
Good mornings
Knee-up
Roman chair crunch

Rehabilitation Workout:
Lower Back Injury

Stretches:
Knee to chest stretch
Alternate knee to chest stretch
Buttock stretch
Spinal push-up
Hamstring stretch on bench
Hip flexor stretch

Exercises:	**Sets x Repetitions**
Stiff-leg deadlift (back rounded)	1-3 x 15-40
Seated row	1-3 x 15-40
Reverse crunch	1-3 x 15-20
Crunch	1-3 x 15-20

Exercises to do cautiously
(may need to use very light weights):
Squat
Stiff-leg deadlift(s)
Overhead press
Upright row
Good mornings
Standing bicep curl
Roman chair crunch

Rehabilitation Workout: Knee Injury

Stretches:
Hip flexor stretch
PNF thigh stretch
Hamstring stretch on bench
Two-leg calf stretch off step

Exercises:	**Sets x Repetitions**
Leg extension (not complete extension)	1-3 x 15-40
Leg curl	1-3 x 15-40
Leg press (when possible)	1-3 x 15-40

Exercises to do cautiously
(may need to use very light weights):

Squat
Stiff-leg deadlift(s)
Good mornings
Standing bicep curl
Standing calf raise
Roman chair crunch

Rehabilitation Workout:
Lower Leg Injury

Stretches:
Two-leg calf stretch off step
One-leg calf stretch off step
Shin stretch

Exercises:	**Sets x Repetitions**
Standing calf raise	1-3 x 15-40
Seated calf raise	1-3 x 15-40
Walk on outsides of feet (each foot)	1-3 x 15-40 steps
Walk on insides of feet (each foot)	1-3 x 15-40 steps

Exercises to do cautiously
(may need to use very light weights):

Squat
Leg press
Leg extension
Leg curl
Any standing exercises

Rehabilitation Workout: Tendinitis

Stretches:
For the muscle connected to the inflamed tendon

Exercises:	**Sets x Repetitions**
Exercises involving muscles connected to the Inflamed tendon	1-3 x 15-40

Exercises to do cautiously
(may need to use very light weights):

Any heavy exercises that involve the injured muscle(s)

Chapter 9

Selected Drugs and Their Effects

*Race enthusiasts who want to be successful, healthy, and have a long
racing career need not take drugs for improved performance.*

As a motorsports enthusiast, you *must* know the substances to stay away from as well as those that may benefit your performance. Many of these substances are obviously drugs. Others are not-quite-so-obvious drugs. Several substances that are commonly used among various athletic competitors can render serious negative side effects.

Drugs are usually prescribed for treat-ment of diseases or trauma. Race enthusiasts who want to be successful, healthy, and have a long racing career need not take drugs for improved performance. All types of athletes (racers included) should be concerned with good training, adequate rest, and smart eating. Attention to these concerns, alone, will help to make you a better racer.

9.1 Alcohol

To some people, drinking a mug of beer is macho. Medical research shows that a very small consumption of alcohol, most notably wine, may aid in the reduction of cholesterol. Small amounts of alcohol have even been shown to increase muscular endurance and strength, although these benefits are very short-lived, for maybe 20min, then problems occur. Other than perhaps an occasional social drink, alcohol has no valuable place in the diet, exercise, or motorsports performance for anyone wanting to be their best.

By consuming alcohol before your strength training or prior to getting behind the wheel of a 700hp machine, you will find it both unproductive and dangerous. In fact, it's nothing short of ignorance.

Since alcohol is a toxin (poison), a number of physical abnormalities can persist. These abnormalities can reduce your muscular strength and endurance, recovery capabilities, aerobic endurance, ability to metabolize fat, and growth of muscle tissue.

Alcohol can also affect your nervous system and brain. Through long-term alcohol use, a severe deterioration of your central nervous system is possible. With short-term use, nerve-muscle interaction can be reduced, resulting in a loss of strength and coordinated movements.

Other dangerous effects include reduced eye-hand-foot coordination and balance, longer periods required for healing, and less efficient healing of injuries. Alcohol can be responsible for a number of sexual dysfunctions as well, including loss of libido (sex drive), reduced sperm formation, menstrual irregularities, and shrinkage of sexual organs. How macho is that?

When alcohol reaches your muscle cells, it can cause damage to them. An inflammation of the muscle cells is common among alcohol drinkers. And when alcohol consumption is practiced for a long time, some of these damaged cells can die, resulting in less functional muscle tissue. In addition, alcohol leaves you with more muscle soreness following training, thus requiring additional time for recuperation.

Alcohol's effects on your heart and circulatory system are numerous. You can experience a reduction in your endurance capacities when you drink alcohol, especially in large quantities. As you consume alcoholic beverages, your heat loss increases because alcohol stimulates your blood vessels to dilate. When the vessels under your skin dilate, heat loss occurs more easily. This can cause your muscles to get cold and, as a result, be slower and weaker during movements.

In addition, alcohol can cause several gastric, digestive, and nutritional irregularities. This drug, which is exactly what it is, causes a release of insulin that will in turn increase the use of glycogen for energy and thus burn less fat for energy. This can result in more difficult fat loss. Since alcohol consumption can interfere with the absorption of many nutrients, it is possible to become anemic and be deficient in several of the B vitamins.

Because your liver is the organ that detoxifies alcohol, the more alcohol you consume, the harder your liver has to work. This additional stress on your liver can damage and even destroy some liver cells.

Alcohol also acts as a diuretic (medication that stimulates the flow of urine). Thus, large amounts of alcohol can place undue stress on your kidneys. Through a diuretic action, your body excretes large amounts of the hormone ADH (anti-diuretic hormone) responsible for slowing the release of urine. This can result in dehydration and subsequent problems dealing with a heated racing machine.

Alcohol is *not* a drink for racers. Its effects on strength, reaction time, skill, vision, and heart function are less than desirable. In fact, alcohol is not a nutritional source of energy even though it contains seven calories per gram. And alcohol's potential for mental deterioration is great, with numerous physical abnormalities possible.

As a speed enthusiast, lay off the alcohol, especially during all types of training and racing competition. And remember, when you do drink alcoholic beverages, your body processes only about 0.5oz an hour. That's usually less than a full serving of beer, wine, or hard liquor.

9.2 Nicotine

Athletes who smoke do not realize the bad effects of their habit. In fact, any athlete who *wishes* to experience success *won't*, if he or she smokes.

The active (and addictive) ingredient in tobacco is nicotine. Although this substance stimulates your adrenal glands for increased energy, the long-term negative side effects by far outweigh any possible benefits.

When you inhale smoke, your heart has to work harder. You can see this by monitoring the pulse of smokers after they inhale a puff on a cigarette. Their heart actually beats faster and harder. In many people who smoke, this effect causes irregular heart contractions that can persist for 30-45min after a "smoke." Together with increased heart rate comes an elevation in blood pressure. Your arteries constrict (get smaller) and cause pressure to build up in them—thus higher blood pressure. These effects also occur in the arteries of your heart, causing less blood flow to the heart muscle. Through prolonged smoking, you can experience difficulty in breathing with the simplest of tasks.

One of the by-products of smoking is carbon monoxide. This substance easily attaches to oxygen molecules and leaves less oxygen available for the working muscles, reducing your endurance tremendously.

The oxygen in your lungs also decreases with smoking by nearly 50 percent.

The numerous toxic by-products of smoking have been associated with cancer, heart disease, and other degenerative illnesses.

Skin temperature can drop due to smoking. This can cause you to feel cold and be less functional during strength training and motorsports competition.

Other forms of tobacco use include smokeless tobacco, which is placed in your mouth. Snuff and chewing tobacco are two forms, and are not without bad side effects. In addition to the nicotine that ends up in your saliva and down your throat, many forms of mouth and lip cancer are caused from these tobacco products.

Tobacco, smoking, and nicotine should not be of any interest for you as a racing enthusiast.

9.3 Caffeine

Surprising to many, caffeine is considered a drug. It is easily obtained in many food products like coffee, tea, chocolate, many soft drinks, analgesics, and some diet aids.

This drug has been proven to stimulate your central nervous system, mobilize free fatty acids, improve muscle contractions, and stimulate the release of various hormones and substrates (chemical compounds) essential to metabolism as well as the rise in the metabolism of carbohydrates for energy. How you *use* caffeine is crucial to the possible benefits it might provide.

If you have a tolerance to caffeine, its use in racing can be beneficial. But if your tolerance to caffeine is low, then its consumption can leave you less than ready for speeds over 55mph.

Reaction time can be improved with caffeine, provided the caffeine is consumed in moderate dosages, say two cups of coffee 1hr before the event. The effect can last for roughly 2-2 1/2hr.

Heavy coffee drinkers who commonly consume two to six cups a day might be forced to stop drinking coffee a few days prior to a race, only so they can get an effect from it when they consume it just prior to the competition. If abstinence is not practiced, reaction time can be unchanged.

Dosages of approximately 3.0 milligrams (mg) of caffeine per kilogram of body weight have been shown to be beneficial. (One cup of coffee can contain anywhere from 40-150mg of caffeine.) Anything less might be unproductive, while more can decrease performance. In fact, caffeine can act as a mild diuretic, causing you to lose valuable body fluids. This can result in dehydration and a host of subsequent problems.

As you may already have experienced, caffeine has the power to reduce drowsiness, increase alertness, and reduce your perception of fatigue. These are some of the stimulating effects of this drug.

For the driver involved in race qualifying, caffeine might get you "up" for it. Research shows that five to six cups of coffee can increase the levels of adrenaline in your blood. Adrenaline is the chemical substance that helps you prepare for intense activity by, among other things, increasing your heart rate, expanding your blood vessels, and increasing your concentration. These attributes are needed in the short-duration, high-intensity driving during qualifying.

For those drivers involved in lengthy races of, say, more than 1hr, caffeine can help through the increased release of free fatty acids and increase the uptake of these fats by your muscles. This results in more energy for enduring muscle work and spares the stored glycogen within your muscles and liver for more intense muscular contractions, when they are called for. The loss of fat is also increased with the use of caffeine before training, since caffeine has been linked with the mobilization of free fatty acids.

It is important to remember, however, that if you are not accustomed to consuming food products containing caffeine, attempting to benefit from their use prior to a race can be either good or bad.

9.4 Anabolic Steroids

It is doubtful that the use of anabolic steroids is widespread among racers and performance driving enthusiasts. However, when one is interested in becoming stronger and having larger muscles, the thought of anabolic steroids may enter one's mind.

Anabolic steroids are synthetic copies of the male-dominant hormone testosterone, which is responsible for building muscle. Regardless of what selected research studies say, anabolic steroids do work. Yes, they contribute to larger and stronger muscles. But the health problems associated with the use of steroids are numerous and well substantiated, therefore discrediting any possible benefits.

There have been an astounding number of stories recounting the undesirable side effects experienced from the use of steroids. Although the long-term effects of steroid use are yet to be discovered, short-term use is linked with several abnormalities.

Psychological problems resulting from steroid use range from increased aggression and violence to mental instability and addiction. Interesting and somewhat controversial is the concern over mental addiction to steroids. When someone taking steroids stops taking them and performance, size, and strength all decrease, a problem occurs. The longer one relies on the "steroid boost," the more difficult it becomes to contend with reduced muscular size and strength. This often results in what can be con-

sidered "steroid abuse"—more are taken and usually in larger dosages.

The physical problems associated with steroid use are vast. Included are high blood pressure, acne, liver disease, gynecomastia (growth under the nipple), heart attack, stroke, and even death. In addition, steroids increase your chances of plaque buildup in the arteries (contributing to heart disease and stroke) and reduce your good cholesterol—high-density lipoprotein cholesterol. Remember, these are only *some* of the bad effects already discovered from steroid use.

Another problem associated with steroid use during strength training is injury. Since testosterone helps to build stronger muscles, and the tendons do not increase in strength to the same degree, the risk of tendinitis is highly increased. No doubt about it, with steroids, the bad outweighs the good.

9.5 Amphetamines

Amphetamines are sometimes used as stimulants. These drugs most often are used to keep people awake or give a boost of energy. They stimulate nervous system action, and subsequently increase your heart rate and blood pressure.

Although amphetamines help to keep you awake and more alert, they can produce major problems in your body. Problems that no driver or pit crew member needs, such as nervousness, insomnia, and anxiety. Racers and crew members may already have enough of these symptoms without taking drugs.

Other possible side effects of amphetamine use include an impaired thermoregulation system of your body. It can become more difficult for your body to tolerate a heated race car as a result of dangerously high body temperatures. In addition, the use of stimulant drugs can produce brain hemorrhages and cardiac failure. These drugs can become addictive, as well.

9.6 Diuretics

People who wish to lose weight often resort to diuretics. These drugs can cause damage to your kidneys and liver, among other vital organs. One of the main problems associated with the use of diuretics is dehydration. As you know, dehydration can lead to several health problems including heart attack and death.

Since the weight you lose with diuretics is simply water weight, you gain it back as soon as you consume liquids. One other problem associated with fluid loss is the increased demand for some minerals regarded as electrolytes. As your body is stimulated to excrete fluids, through the action of diuretics, valuable minerals are lost in the urine. And as a smart eater, you should understand the importance of these nutrients.

Bibliography

Appenzeller, O., and Atkinson, R. *Sports Medicine.* Second Edition. Baltimore-Munich: Urban & Schwarzenberg, 1983.

Astrand, P. O., and Rodahl, K. *Textbook of Work Physiology.* New York: McGraw-Hill, 1970.

Hatfield, F. *Power— A Scientific Approach.* Chicago: Contemporary Books, Inc., 1989.

Hatfield, F. *Ultimate Sports Nutrition.* Chicago: Contemporary Books, Inc., 1987.

Hatfield, F. *Complete Guide to Fitness Training.* International Sports Sciences Association (ISSA), 1991.

Index